Following God Across the Page

A 40-Day Devotional

Alisa Hope Wagner

Following God Across the Page

A 40-Day Devotional

Dedication

God, my Creator, my Savior, my Counselor

Daniel, my high school sweetheart and soul mate

Isaac, my firstborn son

Levi, my brown-eyed boy

Karis Ruth, my cherished girl

Christina, my twin and friend

Thank you to Holly Smith for suggesting the title of this book. Also, I'm so appreciative of Cynthia Faulkner, Shay Lee, Lindsey Plumleigh, Theresa Babcock and Sofia J for supporting Christina at her Botched Reveal. Finally, I'm grateful to Patti Coughlin, Theresa Babcock and Faith Newton for your edits.

Introduction

My identical twin sister was in a near death car accident in 2005. God woke me up in the middle of the night with wrenching stomach pain. Then I heard the phone ring. I knew something tragic had happened. My sister survived after many surgeries, but over the years, her nose began to twist from the inside out. This book is a 40 day devotional on how my writing landed my twin and me on the reality tv show, Botched. Each devotional will encourage your faith with testimonies of God's goodness.

I Don't Know

The yellow visitor sticker clings to
My shirt. I am a visitor in a dream
World of pain and misery, a hell. I
Walk down the white halls into a
White room with sprawled complaining
Bodies, red blood escaping from their
Broken realities. She lies there,
Moaning through dry crusted lips. No
Pill to numb her torture; No off-button
For my life. The doctors and nurses
Deftly dodge the screams of anguish, life
As usual. They are walking reminders
Of my old life, of her old life.
She holds my hand in delirium.
She doesn't Remember.
She won't remember,
but I remember. . . .
She asked the doctor if she
Would live, and he looked at me and
Said, "I don't know."

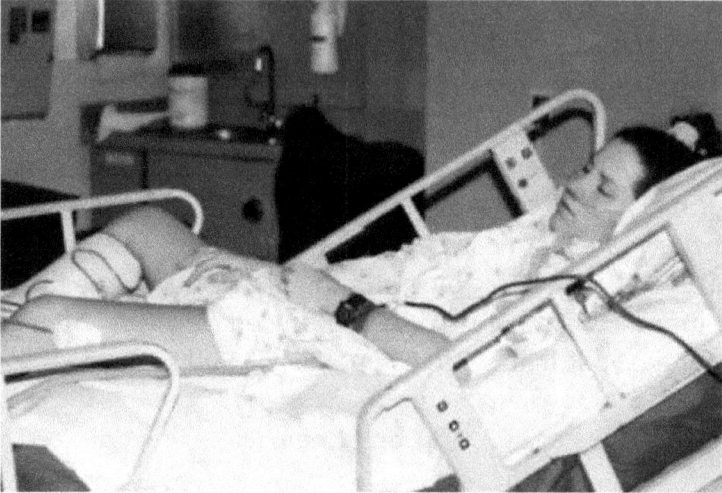

Christina Downing
February 2005

"They triumphed over him by the blood of the Lamb and by the word of their testimony; they did not love their lives so much as to shrink from death" (Revelation 12.11 NIV).

* Watch **Following God Across the Page Book Trailer** at Alisa Hope Wagner's **YouTube Channel** along with her other videos.

You can also watch fun videos from Alisa and Christina's time filming for **Botched on Alisa's My Botched Twin YouTube Playlist**.

Other books in the series: *Following God into the Cage* and **Following God onto the Stage**.

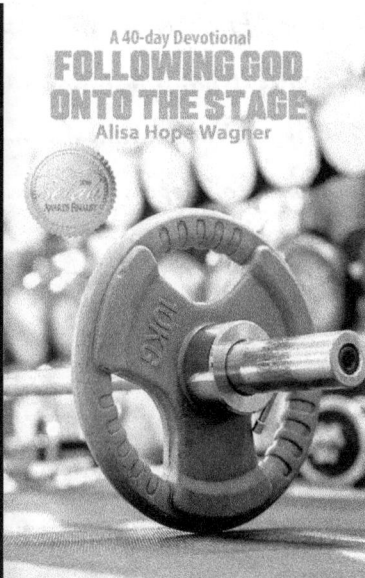

Table of Contents

Day 1: Power in Writing

In February of 2005, my twin sister was in a near death car accident. My husband and I along with our 9-month-old son, drove to the city where they had haloed my sister for trauma surgery. For a few days, I could visit her in the hospital room while my husband stayed in the waiting area with our son. My sister's lungs had collapsed, and the doctors were unable to perform surgery for 10 days. After a while, my husband needed to return to work. I felt helpless to do anything for my sister. I was nursing my son at the time, and I wasn't able to take him with me into the hospital room. No babies are allowed in the rooms for fear their young immune systems will be bombarded with sickness. I couldn't stay with her at nights and try to distract her from the pain. I couldn't help her use the restroom, eat or bathe. I couldn't do any of those things that loved ones desire to do for their recovering family members.

I was honestly frustrated with God. I didn't understand why he allowed this disaster to happen at the worst time possible. I couldn't take care of my sister the way I wanted to. But I just had to do something to show my love for her, so I wrote the story about her car accident and recovery and sent it in to an editor, compiling a book of true life short stories entitled, *God Makes Lemonade*. My submission was published in the book, and my sister's story of overcoming tragedy was shared with others. Little did I know, however, that God would use my gift of writing on behalf of my sister once more. Because of the car accident, the cartilage in her nose was damaged. Slowly over the years, her nose began to twist both inside and out. She went to a local ENT doctor for surgery, but her case was too advance for him, and he was unable to correct her nose.

What could I do to help my sister? Once again, I felt helpless, watching someone I love suffer. I begged God to give me something I could do for her. I went to the computer and did the one thing I knew I was good at: I wrote. I wrote my sister's story, detailing her situation and heartache. I wept as I wrote every sentence because her story was so heartbreakingly true. I then sent her story to a television show called Botched. I used my gift to help someone I loved in need. Many times, we feel like our gifts can't help those around us, but God's imagination is infinite. If He could use a writer to help her sister get corrective nose surgery, He can use anyone's gifting to complete His will on this earth and to fulfill His promises to His Children. He doesn't only use preachers, teachers and leaders; He uses those who are crying out to be used. Cry out to God today, and He will use you in ways you can never imagine.

"God has given each of you a gift from his great variety of spiritual gifts. Use them well to serve one another" (1 Peter 4.10 NLT).

Father, I believe that You have gifted me with talents and abilities that can be used for Your Kingdom and Your Glory. I desperately want to be used by You. I want to make an impact on this earth and the people around me. I want the legacy I leave to be eternal and to bring Your Kingdom into fruition. Guide me to where I need to go and what I need to do. I won't limit Your imagination with trying to know everything. I understand that Your ways are higher than my ways, so I will obediently follow You even when it doesn't make sense in my mind. Please, use me today, Lord. I pray this in Jesus' name, amen.

Questions

1. What gifts do you have that can be used by God?
2. Has God led you to do something that didn't make sense?
3. Was there a time where you felt helpless?

Cry out to be used!

Day 2: Van Tears

My sister was having a particularly bad day in a year filled with difficulty. Her husband had gone oversees for the military and fell in love with someone else, walking away from his marriage of 14 years. She was running a new business. And she was now a single mom of three young kids. On top of it all, she had a twisted nose. As she dropped me off at my house one afternoon, I sat in the passenger seat of her van, listening while she expressed her heartache. I felt like I could do nothing to help her. I couldn't fix her marriage. I couldn't fix her business. And I definitely couldn't fix her damaged nose. When I finally got into my house, I cried out to God, "What can I do for my sister?" I felt the Holy Spirit tell me to write. I walked straight to my computer and did a web search. I remember my sister-in-law telling me a few years back about a show that fixed plastic surgery gone wrong.

My web search instantly led me to the application page for Botched, and I wrote out my sister's story. After over an hour of writing and editing my sister's submission form, I finally sent it. I sat at my computer, feeling better that I got my heartache on paper, but also wondering if I had wasted an hour of my time. I'm always mindful of being a good steward of my time, and I didn't want to waste any moments on something that was not eternally rooted in the Vine of Christ. I went to my prayer closet and grabbed a devotional that I was reading. I opened the book and began to read. The devotional was about Peter chopping off the ear of the High Priest's assistant. Although the injury would not lead to death, Jesus healed his ear (Luke 22.50-51). I felt the Holy Spirit tell me that He was going to use a doctor to heal my sister's deformity. Right then and there I had my word from the Lord, and I put all of my faith on His promise. The reply from Botched took about 6 months to receive, but I would constantly tell my sister to lean on my faith. She would have her surgery!

Before we continue along any path, we must receive a word from the Lord. Many obstacles will come our way and we will be tempted to lose our faith, but if God gives us His "yes," there is nothing that can prevent His will from becoming reality. I know that my sister getting on Botched and having her nose deformity fixed was a long shot, but once I got my "yes" from God, it didn't matter how long it would take or how many people were applying for the show, I knew that she would get that call. Once we get a word from the Lord, we can run with it. Even if the situation seems impossible, we know that all things are possible through God (Romans 8.28). God will make a way when there is no way because if we are rooted in Him, we will bear His fruit to the world.

"I am the vine; you are the branches. If you remain in me and I in you, you will bear much fruit; apart from me you can do nothing" (John 15.5 NIV).

Father, I want everything I do to be committed to You—whether it's work, rest or play—help me to walk in step with Your will and movements. When I seek Your will and I receive a firm word from the Lord, I want to put all my faith into Your "yes." I know that no matter how impossible my circumstances seem that Your Word overpowers them all. I can do all things that You say I can do through the mighty name of Jesus Christ. And I will not let doubt, worry or fear compromise the faith that I have been given. I pray this in Jesus' name, amen.

Questions

1. Do you remember a time that you received a word from the Lord?
2. Have obstacles tried to rob you of your faith?
3. What are you believing God for today?

Believe by Faith!

Day 3: Am I Going to Die?

When I finally arrived at the emergency room where my sister was taken after her car accident, I couldn't believe the state she was in. She was on a gurney in the middle of a large, open white room. There were broken bodies on gurneys all around her. Her hair was matted and her lips were crusted over. She wore a hospital gown, but blood from her accident was still evident all over her body. She writhed in pain and her pupils were fully dilated. The nurses and doctors moved in the daily routine of their job, but it felt like my world had shattered. My sister kept asking me if she was going to die. I would tell her that she was going to live, not die. She would forget only moments later and ask again if she were going to die. I finally asked the doctor moving swiftly by me with his clipboard if my sister would live or not. He simple stated that he didn't know.

For days after my sister continued to ask if she was going to die. The doctors couldn't operate because her lungs had collapsed. They put a metal rod through her femur and dangled a weight on the other end, lifting her femur away from her shattered left hip. The wait was excruciating. It felt like her pain would never end and she would stay hurt and broken forever. This is what it felt like during her divorce. She had a car accident of sorts to her life when her husband left her. It felt like the pain and brokenness would never end. In this life, we have pain and heartache. God never promises us a pain-free life because it is the trials that make us stronger. However, God does promise us that though weeping comes, joy will soon follow (Psalm 30.5). We can trust that God is fully capable of using our pain and heartache for His Righteous Will and not one single tear is shed in vain.

Besides several scars and some nerve damage to my sisters left leg, the only obvious sign from her car accident was her nose deformity. I could never imagine while my sister laid on the gurney in the ER that she would have three kids and a productive life. God healed her body, and now He has healed her nose. And God is continuing to heal her emotional wounds from her divorce. She has wept many tears, but I know that God has them all saved, and He will transform every single one to shouts of joy. If we would only trust God with our pain and heartache and make ourselves vulnerable to His work and care, He will heal us. The healing process may take time, and God may use doctors, therapists, and even twin sisters to carry some of the burden; but His hands will bring healing into our lives.

"For He wounds, but He also binds up; He injures, but His hands also heal" (Job 5.18 NIV).

Father, I know that this life has heartache and pain, but it also has joy and healing. I believe that You will carry me through the hard times and care for me during the healing times. I trust Your will over my expectations. I know that You love me and only want the best for me, and You will use the trials of life to make me spiritually strong and more reliant on You. I will not fear because I know that You are always with me. Jesus died, so I could have a relationship with a Holy God and nothing can take that away. I pray this in Jesus' name, amen.

Questions

1. What difficult time has God asked you to walk through?
2. How did God provide healing after heartache?
3. Name a time when your mourning was transformed to joy?

Joy follows mourning!

Day 4: Two Dinners

My twin and I have done two reality shows together. It's interesting to admit that fact. A producer from the show Made came to our church several years ago. The reality show that normally catered to teens was now trying to produce one for adults. When our pastor announced it, I knew God wanted me to apply. I really didn't want to. The last thing I envisioned for myself was standing in line with everyone else, waiting to talk to the producer. I humbled myself and did what God wanted, and became one of a few people who got to be on the show. I was transformed from a writer to a fighter, and after eight weeks of brutal training, I won my cage fight with a TKO (technical knockout) in a little over a minute. My twin got to be a part of the show, and she supported me while I trained. However, just before my episode aired, the show was canceled. I had worked so hard, but I trusted God with the results. I had this odd sense that I would be on another reality show.

I was not thinking about being on a reality TV show when I submitted my sister's application for Botched. I just wanted her to have some kind of silver lining in her year of heartache. During the six-month wait to see if she was chosen for the show, God gave me many Scriptures to boost my faith. One Old Testament story in particular resonated with me. The Book of Esther details a queen whom God used to save the Israelites. I was intrigued by the two dinners she had with her husband (the king) and Haman (her enemy). During the first dinner, nothing happened. God didn't move, so she requested another dinner. Before the second dinner, God moved profoundly in the heart of the king, and he was ready to respond to Queen Esther's appeal to save her people. Why two dinners? I realized that the first dinner prepared Esther for the second dinner when God would finally move.

My first reality TV show experience prepared me for the one I would do for my twin. During the first one, I felt insecure and I put the show's interest above God's. Reality TV was new to me, and I didn't want to disappoint or offend anyone. I talked about Jesus a lot, but I allowed myself to worry and be anxious about what the production team wanted and thought. During the second show, I knew better. God is the ultimate Authority. He is the One who opens and shuts doors. I knew it was God who was working on behalf of my sister to get her nose fixed. He was revealing His great love for her during her time of trial. I committed to Botched fully aware that God was the One who had chosen my sister, and this time I got to be the one who supported her while the camera was rolling. I realized that many times God gives us a practice round before the real moment arises. He knows the appointment time is significant, so He allows us to have a test run first.

"If you keep quiet at a time like this, deliverance and relief for the Jews will arise from some other place, but you and your relatives will die. Who knows if perhaps you were made queen for just such a time as this?" (Esther 4.14 NLT).

Father, don't let me miss the opportunities that You are presenting me with today. I have experienced in the past disappointments and my expectations were not met, but those times were practice rounds to prepare me for a time of significance and change. I pray for encouragement from Your Word, the Bible. I need my faith boosted from all the times I felt like I walked into a dead-end. I trust that You are orchestrating a mighty move of Your glory, and I want to be ready when the time is right. I want to be used for Your Kingdom Plan, so I will let go of my own expectations. I trust that Your plan is way bigger than what I can think or imagine. I pray this in Jesus' name, amen.

Questions

1. Have you experienced a time when your expectations weren't met?
2. Can you recall God giving you a practice run before the real thing?
3. How is God preparing you for something awesome?

God opens all doors!

Day 5: The Date

I was a little disappointed that my first reality TV episode didn't air, but I knew God wouldn't let it happen without His consent. When the producer told me that they were cancelling the show, he was surprised that I didn't get upset. But I believed that my hard work was not done in vain. I felt God tell me that He was saving my efforts for a different time, and I trusted Him at His word. A few years later, I went to God. I asked Him to give me some ray of hope that He was still holding my efforts in His hands. I had given up all my personal dreams in pursuit of the promises He made me. I didn't want to compromise my faith, but I needed some kind of sign that He was still with me. I felt in my spirit the date, December 23, and right then and there, I placed my faith on that date. There wasn't a doubt in my mind that God would do something amazing on that day.

As the date came closer, I began to get excited. I knew God was about to move! Maybe I would get a publisher. Maybe someone with a platform would share one of my books. Maybe all the years and tens of thousands of hours spent writing for God alone at my computer would finally reap a harvest. I couldn't wait! However, the day came and nothing happened. I was heartbroken. I ran to my prayer closet the next day and prayed to God and asked Him what happened. I felt Him say into my spirit that it was a year too early. I had already waited many years, so I guess I could wait one more. I just begged the Lord to let it be a few days early. I couldn't bear getting to December 23 again without something happening.

The following year, my family and I were on a Disney Cruise just before Christmas. We didn't have Internet connection. Towards the end of the trip, I wondered how my sister was doing. I decided to purchase Wi-Fi just for an hour to catch up with her. When my phone was connected, I instantly received several texts from her. She wrote in caps and lots of exclamation marks that she was chosen to be on Botched. That day was December 21. If I would have waited until our ship ported, I would have received the news December 23. God answered my plea and moved two days early. Watching my sister's story unfold has poured so much power into my faith. I know without any doubt that God is alive, active and attentive to His children. We just need to listen for Him and put our faith in every word He whispers into our spirit.

"For the word of the LORD holds true, and we can trust everything he does" (Psalm 33.4 NLT).

Father, help me to listen while You speak to my spirit. I know the Holy Spirit can share specific details about Your plan with me. I want to read the Bible and pray to You, so I can continually get better at hearing and distinguishing the sound of Your Voice. I know that You desire to be alive, active and attentive in my life. Move mightily in me today. Show me just one small detail of Your plan for my life. I need a vision of what You are trying to accomplish, so I know that I'm on the right path. I understand that You won't reveal everything to me because You want me to have faith, but You do delight in encouraging and motivating me. I pray this in Jesus' name, amen.

Questions

1. What is one thing God has revealed to you?
2. Have you ever been disappointed by a closed door?
3. When has God moved mightily in your life?

Listen for God's voice!

Day 6: Cartwheel Promise

The cartilage in my sister's nose was damaged in her car accident. Over the years, her nose began to twist, making it difficult to breathe. The top of her nose also began to fall to one side. I remember when she noticed the twisting and commented about it. It was such a slow process that I got used to her nose day by day. By the time I really observed it, her nose was clearly deformed. In September 2011, she had corrective nose surgery through insurance by an ENT. She prayed about it and received a word from the Lord. He told her that she would love her nose so much that she would be doing cartwheels. Our sister, Shay, took her to the hospital and kept us informed. It was outpatient surgery, so she came home right after surgery.

A few days later my sister called me with concern. It was obvious to her that the surgery did not work as well as she thought. In fact, over the months her nose began to look worse. She was devastated. How could her nose be worse when God gave her a promise that she would be doing cartwheels? I didn't understand why God was allowing my sister to go through this, but I was certain of this one thing: God always keeps His promises. What we didn't know was that her nose had to get worse before it could get better. When the producers of Botched finally contacted my sister, we were so excited. On the day of her Skype interview, my older sister called me. She got a Timehop from Facebook. The day of the Botched interview would mark five years exactly of the day that my twin had her first corrective nose surgery.

Without the disappointment of the first surgery, my sister would not have received the awesome surgery through Botched. Now she can breathe and she has the most perfect nose. God did fulfill

His promise to her. It was fulfilled five years later. Why did God make her wait? Because He would demonstrate His glory in her life. In the Bible, Jesus was told that Lazarus was sick. Jesus insisted that his life would not end in death. However, Lazarus did die, and Jesus didn't see him until he was buried for 4 days. God must let the promise die in the natural, so He can resurrect it in the supernatural. I can honestly say that my sister's second nose surgery was nothing short of a supernatural miracle. Her new nose is a gift from God, a promise fulfilled, and she does cartwheels knowing that she had been healed according to God's word for her life.

"When he heard this, Jesus said, 'This sickness will not end in death. No, it is for God's glory so that God's Son may be glorified through it'" (John 11.4 NIV).

Father, I know that sometimes our promises need to die in the natural, so You can resurrect them in the supernatural. I will put more faith in Your word for my life than the bleak situation surrounding me. I trust that You are the Creator and You are more powerful than the natural circumstances of this earth. You want to demonstrate Your glory in my life, so I will trust in Your will even though it is not according to my expectations and timetable. Resurrect my promises. Place Your power and Purpose on my life. I want others to see You move mightily in my faith, patience and purpose. I pray this in Jesus' name, amen.

Questions

1. Has a promise of God for your life died?
2. Do you trust that God can resurrect what is dead?
3. How can you revive your faith in God's word for you today?

Your promises will not die!

Day 7: A Family's Help

My twin sister is a single mom of three kids who runs her own business. Leaving for two weeks to film, have surgery and recover took an act of God moving through the lives of our family. I went with my sister to film and help her recover from surgery. My husband became a single dad for two weeks, so he could care for our kids during my absence. My mother watched my sister's kids for almost two weeks, and our older sister was able to watch her kids for a few days when our mom left. Everyone sacrificed and pitched in time, energy and money for Christina to have reconstructive nose surgery. The entire event was a miracle. But that's what family is for. When one person falls, we all reach down and lift her up.

Relationships are so valuable. The first thing God said that wasn't good was for people to be alone (Genesis 2.18). God created us purposefully to need each other. We will never have everything we need alone to fulfill the plans that God has for us. He designed us each with weaknesses and lack which force us to rely on others. God planned for Christina to go on Botched and receive reconstructive nose surgery, but this would have been impossible without her family and friends pitching in. Yes, there is much we can learn, and God does want us to each be accountable for the purposes He has for us. But we will all come to a time when we can't accomplish the next step without someone coming alongside us. We have to be aware of those times, so we can reach out for help when it is needed.

When my sister came home from her surgery, her home was organized and kept up. While her kids were at school during the day, our mom looked around the house and did many things that a husband would do. Before we left, I took my oldest son and got my sister artwork for her living room. Her walls had been blank since the divorce, and I felt God say it was time to replace what was lost. We all reached into my sister's life during a time of emptiness and need and filled a piece of the void with God's tenderness and love. God desires to use His children as blessings to each other. We can act when we know that we are needed and we can do something to help, but we can also receive help when what we need cannot be accomplished alone.

"Two people are better off than one, for they can help each other succeed. If one person falls, the other can reach out and help. But someone who falls alone is in real trouble" (Ecclesiastes 4.9-10 NLT).

Father, help me to know when I'm needed. I want to be able to take a moment and lend a hand, knowing that I can be a blessing in another person's life. I understand that many times You want me to stretch the limits of what I can accomplish, so You expect me to put forth my own effort and strength. But I also realize that there will be times that I won't be able to accomplish Your will alone, and I will have to accept help from others. Thank You for surrounding me with family and friends who will walk alongside of me during times of need. I pray that I can both give and receive help. God, You love when Your children work together to accomplish a purpose greater than themselves. Let me and my family be an example of that love and support. I pray this in Jesus' name, amen.

Questions

1. Has there been a time when you helped a friend or family member?
2. What lack did you have that someone else was able to fill?
3. How can you see God working through your relationships?

Two people are better than one!

Day 8: Waking to Grief

It was the middle of the night when God woke me up. I experienced a great sickening feeling in my stomach, and my heart instantly began to race. Something was seriously wrong. I thought my firstborn son, who was 9 months old, was in danger. I quickly got out of bed and ran to his room. I peered into the crib and saw him sleeping peacefully. I stood there staring at him for several seconds. I still couldn't shake the feeling that something tragic was happening. My stomach was tight, and beads of sweat were forming on the sides of my face. I decided to bring my son to bed with me. I walked through the living room carrying him in my arms. It was dark, but I knew the way well. Right when I stepped under the doorway connecting the living room to the master bedroom, the phone rang. I stopped and shook my head. I knew whatever news was on the other line wasn't good.

I walked to the phone and picked it up. My sister was in a terrible car accident and was being haloed to the state hospital in San Antonio. I immediately fell to me knees and placed my son on the floor next to me. My mind wouldn't comprehend what was happening, and I sat with the phone to my ear, feeling my entire world being swept away by what I just heard. I often wondered why God woke me up before that phone call that late February night. Was it to prepare me? Was it to make sure I didn't miss the call? The experience was so supernatural that I had to conclude it was more than simply a wakeup call. I believe God greatly grieved watching my sister suffer, and because of our mutual love for her, I felt a brief moment of His grief.

God loves us. We are His children. I know from experience that the agony of watching someone you love in pain can be just as heart wrenching as being the one in pain. Many times in the Bible,

Jesus wept over the suffering of the people around Him (John 11.35). How amazing is our God that He would willingly experience heartache with us? He doesn't need us, yet He opens His heart to us and allows Himself to be pulled into both our joys and pains. But just like Jesus dying on the Cross, God can transform that pain and heartache into conduits for His glory. That night when I experienced a moment of God's grief for my sister has since been transformed into rejoicing. I know that this life has pain and heartache, but God knows about every single tear, and He will not let them fall in vain.

"You keep track of all my sorrows. You have collected all my tears in your bottle. You have recorded each one in your book" (Psalm 56.8 NLT).

Father, I'm in awe that You would walk with me during the hard times and the good. You rejoice when I rejoice. You grieve when I grieve. Help me to recognize that because of Jesus' Finished Work on the Cross, I can now have Your Spirit in me, the Holy Spirit. And the Holy Spirit knows what I am going through and experiences my heartache with me. How amazing it is to have a God who truly understands me. I never want to take Your presence for granted. You paid the price of Your Son, Jesus, in order to have a relationship with me. Thank You for loving me so much that You would reach down into my despair in order to bring beauty out of my ashes (Isaiah 61.3). I pray this in Jesus' name, amen.

Questions

1. Was there ever a time when God comforted you?
2. Do you know that God is with you during good and bad times?
3. How does feeling God's presence help you through trials?

God weeps and rejoices with you!

Day 9: The Burden of Hope

When I submitted my sister's application to Botched, I didn't tell her right away. Her emotions were raw from her recent divorce, and she was so busy with her kids and work that I didn't want to add to her stress. She had already accepted her nose as her current fate, and I needed to be careful reopening old wounds. I still recognized God's "Cartwheel Promise" to her many years back, so my faith was set on her nose being corrected and healed. I waited to give her the news until the producers reached out via email. By then, she had to get involved with phone and skype interviews. But I knew that it was time to reopen the old wound because God was about to perform a miracle of healing on her behalf.

Reopening old wounds is not something new. There was a certain wealthy woman in the Bible who never had children. She allowed the Prophet Elisha to stay in one of the rooms in her home. One day, Elisha told this woman that in one year she would have a son. The first thing the woman cried out when he told her this was, "Oh man of God, don't deceive me and get my hopes up like that!" (2 Kings 4.16 NLT). Sometimes our greatest hopes can become our most difficult burdens. It is often easier to bury the dream than to carry the weight of it. We all hold the burden of our promises, and when they seem to die, sometimes we say goodbye instead of waiting on God. But when God begins to move, we mustn't resist Him. We can let Him into our broken dreams, trusting that He can breathe life into them.

We all have promises that we are waiting on. God promised me many years ago that my writing would be used for His glory and to bring many people closer to the Lord. God knows that carrying the weight of His promises can cause us heartache, but He also knows that at the end of our wait is not just a single blessing, it is a Tree of Life of Blessings! Jesus is the Beginning and End of our promises, the Founder and Perfecter (Revelation 22.13 and Hebrews 12.2). He whispers them into our hearts and links them to the foot of His throne. As we chase after each one, we are brought closer and closer into His likeness. That's what promises are for—they bring us on paths that shed us of our selfishness and transform us from one glory to the next (2 Corinthians 3.18). So let God reopen your dreams, and see where they take you!

"Hope deferred makes the heart sick, but *when* the desire comes, *it is* a tree of life" (Proverbs 13.12 NKJV).

Father, I don't want to give up on my dreams. I know that carrying their weight is difficult, but I trust that the eternal blessings will be greater than my suffering. Reveal Your promises to me today, and remind me of ones that I might have buried too soon. Resurrect my destiny, so I can run my race to win. I want my life to have purpose and meaning, and I know that only through You can I attain them. Use my dreams to shape me into my best self, changing from glory to glory into the image of Your Son, Jesus. I will no longer compromise the faith I once had in the promises You have given me! I pray this in Jesus' name, amen.

Question

1. What promise has God given you that you may have forgotten?
2. Has God resurrected a promise for which you waited with faith?
3. How can you chase your destiny today?

Don't give up on your dreams!

Day 10: Hospital Redemption

When my sister had her car accident, my son was only 9 months old. I couldn't care for her before or after her surgery or while she recovered, so I wrote her story instead. Writing her story gave me a small comfort knowing that I was able to show her how much I cared; however, I still felt like I missed out on being there for her when she needed me most. I wanted to be able to stay with her during the night and help her go to the restroom, to bathe, to wash her hair, to get dressed—all the basic actions people with serious injury struggle with. During the time my sister spent in California for her reconstructive nose surgery, God gave me the opportunity to take care of her like I had wanted.

After my sister's surgery, she went to a recovery hospital overnight. My sister was in a lot of pain, and I couldn't wait to be at her side. I was determined to help her use the restroom, feed her, bathe her, blow dry her hair and do all things caregivers do. As I was settling into my sister's room, a nurse told me that the room was too small for a pull away bed, so I couldn't stay with her that night. I couldn't believe it. I asked them if there was any way I could be with my sister. I promised I was simply there to help her and that I wouldn't get in the way. They said there was nothing they could do. The room was too small. I cried, but I knew God was ultimately in control. I still had a few more visiting hours left, so I spent time unpacking my sister's suitcase and feeding her the dinner they brought to her room.

I was so heartbroken. I finally was getting the opportunity to care for my sister when she really needed me, but now I had to leave. But just before I left, the owner of the hospital came into my sister's room. He asked my sister if she wanted me to stay, and she emphatically nodded her head. He looked at me and said that there was an empty room next to her room. When he offered it to me, I couldn't help but feel so grateful. I spent the night in my room with the door wide open. Anytime I heard my sister's voice, I was at her side. I helped her use the bathroom, take her medicine, blow dry her hair, get dressed and all the other things that she needed. I even jumped out of my bed several times thinking I heard her voice, but she was sound asleep. I felt so honored to serve her, and I knew that God was redeeming the time that I couldn't be there for her.

"The LORD will fight for you; you need only to be still" (Exodus 14.14 NIV).

Father, I trust that You are fighting on my behalf. I want to serve You and be a blessing to others. You know my heart's desires, and You will move in the hearts of others to accomplish Your Kingdom Plan. When I base my desires on Your purposes, I can have faith that You will accomplish them. I don't have to be anxious or worried about the circumstances around me because You will finish in me all that You set out to achieve. Help me to be calm and peaceful even when situations don't go my way. I believe that You will provide for me right when I need it most. I pray this in Jesus' name, amen.

Questions

1. How has God provided when You needed Him most?
2. Have you experienced God moving in the hearts of others?
3. What worry can You give to God, trusting that He can handle it?

Trust God to provide!

Day 11: Emotional Wounds

We all get emotional wounds in life. The people around us hurt us and leave gaping sores that, if not treated and healed right away, can become weeping wounds. These weeping wounds will eventually affect every aspect of our lives. The Bible says that people are like sandpaper, smoothing out our rough edges. However, if we have weeping wounds even the slightest touch can be painful. My sister received a large, open wound when her husband divorced her. The process of divorce was extremely painful and left her feeling rejected and abandoned. However, she was so busy being a single mom of three and running a business that she was unable to really mourn her loss and let God cleanse and bandage her wounds.

When we went to Los Angeles to film for the Botched episode, my sister had no choice but to deal with her pain. Although she was there to get her nose corrected and healed, God was able to deal with her emotional injuring as well. Christina was surrounded by producers and film people who genuinely cared about her story. The film team even teared up when she expressed her pain. She was surrounded by so much love, empathy and understanding. It was like God was wrapping her up in a soft blanket, telling her it was time for her to deal with her heartache. God used every person like a sterile cloth, wiping the bitterness away from her emotional wound. She is now on the road to healing, resting in the truth that God loves her and wants to make her whole again.

In the Old Testament, people with weeping wounds were separated from the society (Leviticus 13.45-56*).* The unhealed wounds would become infected and ooze over everything these people touched. Today, many people carry around emotional weeping wounds that they have not let God heal. They either keep picking at the scab, reinjuring themselves over and over again by reliving the moment, or they allow bitterness to set in. Either way, they can't have interactions with others because normal human contact hurts them. Eventually, they ostracize themselves from the community around them. All their relationships are tainted by their wounds that continue to fester. When we receive an emotional wound, we must know that it will not heal overnight, but we need to start the process of healing right away. God can cleanse and bandage our wounds, but we need to be open to the process, trusting that God loves us and wants to heal us.

"As iron sharpens iron, so a friend sharpens a friend" (Proverbs 27.17 NLT).

Father, please search me and know my heart. Do I have weeping wounds that may be affecting my relationships and life? I know that in this life, we will have the normal bumps and scrapes from relationships, but I also understand that there will be times that people will wound us deeply. Show me how I can heal those wounds. I want you to cleanse them and bandage them, so I can continue the process of healing. Bring people and resources to me to help me in my process of healing. I want to rest in Your Arms, knowing that You will make me whole again. I pray this in Jesus' name, amen.

Questions

1. Do you have any deep emotional wounds that need to be healed?
2. Are you easily hurt or offended by everyday interactions?
3. Has there been a time when you went through the process of healing?

Let God cleanse and heal your wounds!

Day 12: The Bell

During our first interview, I talked about how I wanted to care for my sister after her surgery. I explained that during her car accident, I couldn't be there for her. This would be a redemption for me of sorts. One of the doctor's suggested that I buy my sister a bell, so she could ring it whenever she needed me. This was stated mainly as a joke, but it became one of the plot lines of the episode. The morning of the surgery, the producer texted, asking if I had found a bell yet. I couldn't believe it. I didn't think the bell would become so important. But God knew that I needed a distraction during my sister's nine-hour surgery. After I brought my sister into the skilled hands of the plastic surgeon, I went off to Rodeo Drive to find a bell. Finding a bell on such a notoriously expensive street sounded ridiculous, but the street was walking distance from our hotel. I had nowhere else to go, so I set out on my journey to find the impossible.

As I walked past the busy shops, I looked in every door for a customer bell I could bribe a clerk to sell to me. I also called local hardware stores. They said they had the brass office desk bells, but that was not what I envisioned for my sister. I felt the Holy Spirit tell me not to compromise. He was going to help me find my bell. I stopped at a chocolate store to purchase chocolates for the doctor. I was talking to different store salespeople on the phone while I waited in line, asking each of them if they had a bell to sell. A woman in the chocolate store overheard me and said that I should try Saks Fifth Avenue. I walked to the store, realizing that time was getting late. I needed to get back to the hospital, but I still hadn't found a bell. Again, I felt the Holy Spirit say, "I got this. Don't compromise your faith." I went into Saks Fifth Avenue and asked for their kitchen department, but that location didn't have one.

I walked out of the store, knowing that I needed to head back. I looked across the street and saw a consignment shop that had furniture, dishes and other home goods. I hurried to the store and asked the clerk if they had a bell. She said she might have one, and we began to search the store. Finally, there in a glass case was my sister's bell. It was a crystal dinner bell and it was only twenty dollars. Thank the Lord! The bell was giftwrapped, and I couldn't help but kiss it! God had answered my prayers. I didn't have to buy a cheap office bell or a sterling silver bell from Cartier (which was my last desperate thought). I got my sister the perfect bell. And was reminded that if we can have faith for little things like a bell, God can take care of our biggest heart's desire. We simply need to hold onto our faith and trust that God will do what He says He will do!

"Take delight in the LORD, and he will give you the desires of your heart" (Psalm 37.4 NIV).

Father, thank You for helping me not to compromise my faith. You had something special picked out for my sister, and I am so grateful that I listened to the Holy Spirit's promptings in my heart. God, You have all the world's resources at Your disposal, and there is nothing beyond Your imagination or reach. Help me to line myself up with Your will because I know that only through You can my life embrace amazing and eternally significant occurrences. I pray this in Jesus' name, amen.

Questions

1. When have you been tempted to compromise your faith?
2. How has God shown up in your life in an amazing way?
3. Is there something right now that you're believing God for?

Don't compromise your faith!

Day 13: Tricking Twins

When my twin sister and I went to our first filmed interview with the doctors, we were super nervous. There is a plethora of details to think about: What am I going to wear, what am I going to say, what will the doctors think, will I breakdown and cry, etc. I tried really hard not to let worry take over my thoughts, but it was difficult not to feel the normal stage jitters. When we arrived at the filming location, the producers let me know that I would be going in first to meet the doctors alone. We were going to try to trick the doctors into thinking that I was the one in need of reconstructive nose surgery. When I received this news, I thanked God I didn't know it any sooner. I would have stayed up all night, thinking about having to be filmed first. I would have lost my peace and joy, and fear and fret would have infiltrated my every attitude and thought on camera.

Many times, God keeps information from us to prevent us from worrying. But He'll reveal it to us right when it's necessary for us to know. He knows that sometimes we try to wield our control over the situation instead of simply resting in our trust in God's timing. We consume all of our energy, trying to dig up every single detail of what's going on, and then we wonder why our peace has left us. Why should we worry about the problems of tomorrow today (Matthew 6.34)? With our access to so much information via the Internet, it is easy for us to find something to worry about. We can become so enthralled with what's going on around us that we forget that we have our own life and our own daily struggles to focus on.

Sometimes knowing everything is not good for us. God gives us grace to meet the heartache of our lives. But when we are consuming information that is not meant for us, we will not receive God's grace to match it. We must be very careful what we allow our hearts to feed on. We are not Jesus; we were not meant to take on all the world's problems. If we find ourselves burdened with social media or the news, maybe we should take a break from consuming information for a while. God has given us just enough grace to handle the relationships and trials in our immediate sphere of influence. He has given us peace and strength for today's information only. If we feel stressed out or overwhelmed, we should give the control back to God. Only He deserves to be in charge. He will protect us from information that we don't have the grace to handle.

"Above all else, guard your heart, for everything you do flows from it" (Proverbs 4.34 NIV).

Father, please help me to learn to trust the flow of information that You allow in my life. I don't want to consume details from the news and/or social media that is not meant for me. Help me to let go of always trying to control everything. I don't want to be burdened by information that I don't have the grace to carry. I want to guard my heart, so I trust that You will withhold information from me that is not necessary for me to know. And when it is time for me to perceive certain details, I know You will give me the grace to endure the knowledge. I don't want to live in ignorance, but I do want to live in peace. So I trust You to guide what my ears hear, my eyes see and my mind understands. I pray this in Jesus' name, amen.

Questions

1. Have you ever been burdened with information you had no grace for?
2. Is it easy or difficult for you to give up control?
3. Is social media and/or the news burdening you with information?

Guard your heart!

Day 14: A Seed

I had totally forgotten that it was my sister-in-law who told me about Botched during its first season. I must have been talking about my sister's nose and her reconstructive surgery that didn't work. I can now recall her saying that I should try to apply my sister for the show, but I had immediately refused the idea. I knew my sister was uncomfortable with airing her problems, and she would never want to do a show where she had to be vulnerable to the world. However, God knew that circumstances would change, and my sister would finally get to a point where she would reach out for help. My sister's life had been devastated by divorce, and her nose continued to get worse. By the time I sent her application into Botched, she was ready to take the leap into reality TV and plastic surgery again.

The seed of Botched that my sister-in-law planted inside of me laid dormant for several years. It wasn't until I saw my twin sister crying in her van that it resurfaced. I thank God that the seed was planted, so it could sprout at just the right time. God knew the seed was hidden just beneath the surface, waiting for the time He would water it with the move of His Spirit. Many of us have seeds that others have planted in us. They are right now lying dormant in our subconscious just waiting for a time that they are watered. God plants seeds of destiny in us, and He is waiting for the right time to water them. We must be aware of God's movements, so we will be ready when the seed sprouts. If I hadn't written Botched right then and there when the seed was watered and sprouted, I might have totally missed the opportunity to be a part of God's promises in my sister's life.

God also uses us to plant seeds of salvation into others. There are people around us who do not have Jesus as their Lord and Savior, so they cannot have a relationship with God. The gift of salvation is the most important seed that we can plant in people. I write about Jesus almost every day because I want people to know Jesus Christ and receive the gift of salvation. Although I have no idea how my writing influences others, I scatter my little seeds of salvation as often and as far as possible. I pray that they get lodged into people's subconscious, and one day someone will come along and water them. Then salvation can sprout, and I will get to meet them in heaven. The seeds we scatter may not seem like much, but we may never know what harvest can come from one little seed when God makes it grow!

"I planted the seed in your hearts, and Apollos watered it, but it was God who made it grow. It's not important who does the planting, or who does the watering. What's important is that God makes the seed grow" (1 Corinthians 3.6-7 NLT).

Father, I want to be aware of the seeds of destiny that You have planted inside of me. I want to feel when You water one and when it springs up, so I can allow You to grow and tend it. I don't want to be so busy and rushed that I miss all that You are cultivating inside of me. Also, help me to share seeds of salvation with others. I know that You designed me uniquely to share the Good News of Jesus Christ in specific ways. I may not be a pastor or a teacher, but I can share what I've learned to the people You have placed in my life. I pray this in Jesus' name, amen.

Questions

1. What is one seed of destiny that God has planted inside of you?
2. Can you sense God's harvest growing around you?
3. How can you plant a seed of salvation today?

Let God water the seeds inside of you!

Day 15: Gathering Photos

God created me to be very nostalgic. My melancholy, reflective mood makes me a good writer, but it also causes me to be sentimental when it comes to my family. Because of my sentimental nature, I take a lot of photos. Even before digital, I would organize and save photos from my childhood and teen years. I manage a private family blog with photos and descriptions about our daily life. I've kept this blog for over ten years now, and every month I give several hours to uploading our memories. When my family and I go on big trips, I also organize and purchase a hard copy photo album of the event. They are like coffee table books of nostalgia. After my sister's car accident many years ago, I made a homemade booklet for our family with photos, words and poems of what she went through. I feel deeply and analyze everything, so the activity of writing and taking photos helps me to process and discern what I'm feeling.

When I sent my sister's application into Botched, they requested lots of photos. They wanted to see her nose before the car accident and after, and before her first nose surgery and after. They wanted childhood photos, teen year photos, family photos and activity photos. I gathered them all and sent them to my sister. After her second reconstructive nose surgery was finished, and the production team was working on her episode, more photos were required. Thankfully, I have kept all my photos in organized hard drives through the years. This time I sent photos of Christina's car accident. I sent photos of her in a wheelchair, in crutches, doing physical therapy and photos showing all her scars. One of the producers said that I was one of the most thorough picture gatherers that they've ever experienced. I couldn't help but muse that God made me that way for such a purpose.

God gives us each passions and talents, and they can be used for both our public and personal lives. My gift of nostalgia is definitely used for my public writing, but it also shapes me as a mother, wife, sister and daughter. God will bring circumstances in our lives that will allow us to use the talents He has given us. He knows how to bring the best out of each of us, and He will allow the needs around us to cultivate our abilities. Our passions will normally be exposed in our personal lives first. When we become well acquainted with using our talents at home, God will then anoint those talents to influence the public sphere for His glory. Our family and friends get to be the initial observers and benefactors of what we are capable of achieving, and they can become our biggest supporters of how God uses our abilities in the public realm.

"Your hands have made me and established me; Give me understanding and a teachable heart, that I may learn Your commandments" (Psalm 119.73 AMP).

Father, I want to use my gifts and talents for my family in the sphere of my home life. I can serve the people closest to me while cultivating the abilities that You have given me. My family should be well-acquainted with my passion and purpose before You unleash me to serve a need in a public atmosphere. I ask for guidance while using my talents. I want everything I do to be rooted in You, so my efforts can be eternal. Help me to serve my family first, so they can become my biggest cheerleaders in all I do for Your Kingdom. I pray this in Jesus' name, amen.

Questions

1. What is one talent that God has given you?
2. How can you use your passions in your home?
3. Has God showed you how to use your talents?

God has designed you for a purpose!

Day 16: Skilled Surgeon

From the first moment that I sent in my sister's application to Botched, I unknowingly carried a burden. Without realizing it, I began to feel pressure to ensure her second reconstructive nose surgery was a success. I had started the Botched Ball rolling, and I wanted everything to go well. My priority concern was my sister's health. I know with any surgery, there are risks involved. I didn't want anything to happen during anesthesia or the surgery itself to cause harm to her. My second concern was with my sister's nose. She had already experienced a giant letdown from her first nose surgery, and I did not want that to happen again. Her nose deformity greatly diminished her quality of life both in how she breathed and how she felt about herself. I had faith that God was going to fulfill His promises to her, but there were so many unknowns.

When we finally sat down to talk with the doctors, I could feel a smile spread across my face. The doctor described my sister's nose complications, and he explained how he could help her with assured words. Although I didn't understand much of his medical terminology, I could tell he knew what he was talking about, and he was confident that he could help her situation. I was finally able to let go of the burden that I had unconsciously accepted. Hearing the doctor describe the solution for my sister's nose deformity gave my faith a huge boost. I knew that God would be using this doctor to achieve His promises for my sister, and I could rest in the awareness that God would oversee every detail of her surgery and recovery. God had called this doctor to carry the weight of my sister's surgery, but he carried it with ease because it suited his calling and abilities.

There is nothing wrong with placing our confidence in the hands of capable people whom God is using to further His Kingdom on earth as it is in heaven. If God has designed them for a specific purpose, then the weight of that purpose will not be too heavy for them. We can place our confidence in pastors to bring a word from the Lord, we can place our confidence in airline pilots to fly the plane, we place our confidence in counselors to guide our understanding, and we can place our confidence in doctors to repair our body. God can and will use His Children to be conduits of His grace, favor and blessing to the world. God can achieve His purposes with or without our help, but He is so loving and wise that He willingly allows people to carry small parts of His Kingdom Plan to fruition. We can cast our cares on God, trusting that He can work through the abilities of others to accomplish His will.

"For God is working in you, giving you the desire and the power to do what pleases him" (Philippians 2.13 NLT).

Father, I know that You are orchestrating Your Kingdom Purposes on earth, and You allow us to play a small, but valuable role in all that You are accomplishing. Help me not to unconsciously carry the weight of burdens that I can do nothing to alleviate. Bring people into my life who You can use to accomplish Your promises in my life and the lives of my family and friends. I know that all people are fallible, but You can still achieve Your Perfect Will through them. I place all my faith in You, but I'll also pour confidence into the people that You have purposefully chosen to achieve specific aspects of Your Plan. I pray this in Jesus' name, amen.

Questions

1. Has God blessed you through the abilities of someone else?
2. How can God use you to bless others?
3. Are you unknowingly carrying the weight of an outcome?

God will use others to achieve His Plan!

Day 17: Borrowed Clothes

I over packed for our trip to Los Angeles to film for Botched. I knew that Los Angeles weather can be finicky during the winter—bright and sunny one day and dreary and cold the next—so I wanted to be prepared. I also knew that reality TV has many clothing regulations. I brought lots of jeans, shoes, shirts, jewelry, workout clothes and jackets. Once I got the color requirements from the show, I went shopping. I bought all the jewel tones that they were requesting. I found shirts for myself and for my sister, knowing that she probably wouldn't make it out to the mall. I shoved so much stuff into two bags that they both reached their capacity. My sister, on the other hand, didn't have time to really worry about her wardrobe. She packed what she needed, and we headed out to Los Angeles.

For almost each day of filming, my sister wore one of my shirts. I knew she was the focal point of the episode, so it was more important for us to prepare her outfits first. The shirt that I had planned on wearing to my green screen interview, she wound up wearing to meet the doctors. The shirt I brought for after our workout session, she wore while meditating. The shirt I bought at the mall, she wore to her green screen interview. She wore my jewelry, boots and anything else she needed. This was her moment, and my suitcases were at her disposal. But since I looked out for my sister, God looked out for me. He made sure that I looked nice too. It's interesting that since I let my twin have free access to my suitcases, I wore outfits that I would have never considered. And when I look back at filming, I'm so pleased with the ensembles that I chose. I also went to the mall and bought us a few matching outfits to wear during and after my twin's surgery, as a demonstration of our close relationship.

Because I placed the focus on serving rather than taking, God was able to take care of both my sister's and my wardrobe. We both dressed well. The Bible says that if someone asks something of us, we should give it (Luke 6.30). This doesn't mean that we let people walk all over us and take whatever they want. We first need to be careful about who we let into our lives. But if there is someone in need and we have the capacity to give, we can offer it freely, trusting that God will continue to bless us. God blessed me with the ability to buy clothes, so there was no reason I shouldn't share what I had been given with my sister. All blessings come from the Lord anyway. My sister and I found ourselves in a special situation that called for team work! God was orchestrating a unique move of His Spirit, and we needed to be dressed for the occasion.

"Every good and perfect gift is from above, coming down from the Father of the heavenly lights, who does not change like shifting shadows" (James 1.17 NIV).

Father, I know that everything good comes from You. I want to hold loosely to what You have given me, knowing there may come a time when You'll want me to pay that blessing forward. I would rather have treasures in heaven than all the wealth of the world. I don't want people to trample over me, but I also don't want to miss out on being a blessing to others. Help me listen closely to the Holy Spirit's move in my life, so I can give, receive and steward the blessings that You are arranging. I pray this in Jesus' name, amen.

Questions

1. Have you ever given something that you loved?
2. When has God asked you to put someone's interest first?
3. How has God blessed you after you gave to others?

Every good gift comes from God!

Day 18: Strong Home

Going to Los Angeles put pressure on my family. I had never left home for so long, and I prayed to God for strength to endure being without them. I felt the Holy Spirit tell me that the time separated from my family would go by quickly and soon enough it would be over. In retrospect, the time did speed by and I enjoyed pouring into my relationship with my sister. However, there were nights during our stay in Los Angeles that both she and I ached to be home with our kids. God used those two weeks to orchestrate an amazing miracle in my sister's life, and I'm glad I was able to be a part of something so special. I realize, though, that it was only because my home life was so healthy that my family could bear the weight of my absence for so long.

My home life is important to me because it is extremely important to God. God created the family, and He instituted the family as the cell of our civilization. I serve, cultivate and nourish my family, and I feel God's immense pleasure in my ministry as wife and mother. If my family were emotionally and spiritually malnourished because of my carelessness or indifference as a mother and wife, there would be no way I could have left for two weeks without causing great strain. Only a flourishing family would be strong enough to tolerate such absence and not be drastically affected by it. I have a harvest of fruit in my family life from years of obedience, service and enjoyment.

People desire to make an impact on the world around them. They want God to use them to make a difference for His Kingdom and Glory. However, if they are not caring for the family that He has blessed them with, why would He expand their borders to the public world? Having public influence can place great pressure on a family. I believe pressure is a good thing that helps us grow, learn and change; but if the family is not fully functioning, then the pressure will break the family, not grow it. Before we make a choice to do something that would be a burden to our families, we need to make sure that God is giving us His approval. If we have been neglecting our role as parent and spouse, God may keep our borders small until we have shown ourselves as faithful stewards of our family first. But if our family relationships are solid, He will broaden our borders, knowing we can handle the burden with the blessing.

"But if anyone does not provide for his relatives, and especially for members of his household, he has denied the faith and is worse than an unbeliever" (1 Timothy 5.8 ESV).

Father, I am so thankful for the family You have given me. I want to be a good steward of the souls You have placed in my life. I desire to be good to my spouse, daily meeting the needs of my marriage. I adore my children, and I don't take being their parent lightly. I know that You love Your children so much that You died for them, and You take pleasure in my joy to serve them. I want my family to thrive, and I long to be surrounded by the fruit of my labor. When there is additional pressure on our family, I know it will bring us closer together and closer to You. I pray this in Jesus' name, amen.

Questions

1. Was there a time that your family had extra pressure placed on it?
2. Do you see fruit in the relationships of your family?
3. How can you cultivate your family today?

God loves family!

Day 19: Sore Muscles

For part of our Botched episode, Christina and I had to work out. I'm a certified trainer and have written books about faith and fitness, so the producers wanted me to show how I exercise with my sister. They wanted us to run steps located in a neighborhood near the Hollywood sign. Los Angeles is full of hills, so these steps were steep. We ran up and down them several times while the cameras were rolling. It was a great work out, but I knew we would be sore the next day. Although my sister and I both exercise daily, the steepness of the stairs and the exuberance of our run exhausted our muscles. Thankfully, we filmed our work out scene on Friday, so we had the weekend to recover from the run before Christina's surgery on Monday.

Because of Christina's hip fracture and nerve damage in her left leg, her calf was extremely sore the next day. In fact, it cramped throughout the entire weekend. I continually rubbed her calf, trying to get the muscle to loosen up. I wanted to move the waste material out of the muscle, so massage, light walking and lots of water was in order. During this time, I had also gotten a slight fever because we had run steps in the cold. California weather can be unpredictable, and I packed exercise clothes for warm weather, not cold. I couldn't help but be a little frustrated. How could so much be happening to us just before my sister was having extensive nose surgery? We rested up over the weekend, doing absolutely nothing that would compromise our muscles and health further. By Monday morning we were back to normal and ready for surgery day and the following days of recovery.

I've gotten used to the reality that many trials will occur just before God is about to move mightily. My sister was about to have corrective nose surgery after years of waiting for God's promises to be fulfilled, and it seemed that everything was going against us. She needed to be well to have surgery, and I needed to be well to help her recover. But we must expect many things to go wrong when we are walking down the right path. The problems that arise when we are dedicated to doing God's will should never discourage us, though. They should not become a reason for us to give up. Once we know the direction God has for us, we should expect trials to come against us. These trials don't have to be stumbling blocks because we know that God can use them as stepping stones of resolve and commitment. So don't be surprised when you start pursuing God's promises by the mountains that stand in your way. Jesus said that all you need to have is faith and those mountains will be cast aside.

"Truly I tell you, if anyone says to this mountain, 'Go, throw yourself into the sea,' and does not doubt in their heart but believes that what they say will happen, it will be done for them" (Mark 11.23 NIV).

Father, I realize that the path to achieving my promises will be filled with roadblocks. I will not let those trials discourage me or make me give up. I know that trials will be thrown my way, but You are greater and stronger than all of my setbacks. I want to rely on You, God, because only through You is my victory sealed. I can achieve my destiny despite the hardships along the way, knowing that You are always for me. I pray this in Jesus' name, amen.

Questions

1. What trials stand in the way of your promises?
2. Have hardships ever caused you to give up?
3. Do you know that your victory is secure in God?

Make those stumbling blocks your stepping stones!

Day 20: Jesus Talk

During the first reality show I filmed, I talked about Jesus a lot. I tried to lead one of my producers to Jesus. I talked about Jesus to everyone on the show. I felt like I needed to constantly be "shining my light" into the darkness, but I may have been a little blinding with my constant talking. There is absolutely nothing wrong with being a light and presenting the Good News of Jesus Christ, but I realize now that I should have relied more on the move of the Holy Spirit than the moving of my own mouth. God has an amazing ability to prepare people's hearts for the Gospel, much like soil is prepared for seed. Instead of listening to the Holy Spirit, I just went into Jesus overdrive. I've since learned to be sensitive to the Holy Spirit. He will guide my words to say the right things at just the right time.

So for the Botched Reality TV show, I tried to not squeeze the Gospel into every sentence I spoke. But instead of waiting for the right time, I felt myself go completely mute. Now I felt nervous, and I was constantly thinking about whether I should mention God or not. I was so anxious about my words that I missed several opportunities to be a light. The night after the first day of filming, I felt God's conviction. He wasn't trying to shame me (although I shamed myself); rather, He was trying to rid me of my nervousness. I felt God tell my spirit that I went from one extreme to another. Instead of overthinking it, I simply needed be open and available for whenever the Holy Spirit wanted to use me to speak His truth. I determined myself that the next day, I would simply rest in God's capable hands. If I remained sensitive to the Holy Spirit, He would speak through me at the right time (Luke 12.11)

While we filmed the following morning, I put my worries on the Lord. Whether I remained quiet or spoke up would be completely up to Him. I just made myself available to His move. At one point during the day, my sister became very vulnerable with her heartache in front of the camera. There were many issues that she hadn't dealt with, and the show was allowing her to work through wounds that she had been carrying. I felt the Holy Spirit instantly move through my words. I told her that her value was not based on how she looked or what she did; rather, her value came from simply being a child of God. This truth is so counterculture in a world that allows our looks and careers to define our worth. But God's ways are not our ways, and He places great value on us despite what we look like or what we do. I believe many people need to hear this truth. Instead of trying to earn love, we can embrace the truth that we are loved.

"In the same way, let your light shine before others, that they may see your good deeds and glorify your Father in heaven" (Matthew 5.16 NIV).

Father, I trust that You will speak through me. I will not worry about what I'm going to say and when I will say it. If I stay sensitive to the Holy Spirit's move, You will give me the right words at the right time. You love people, God. And I know that You will prepare their hearts for the Good News found in Jesus Christ. I give my anxieties to You, and I trust that You will speak through me. I pray this in Jesus' name, amen.

Questions

1. Have you ever felt embarrassed about telling others about Jesus?
2. Do you remember a time when God spoke to you through others?
3. How has God spoken through you to encourage someone else?

Don't worry about what you will say!

Day 21: Riding Backseat

Los Angeles is a big city with lots of traffic. Luckily, there is a car service of people who use their cars to take visitors to different destinations within the city. This service is like the taxi industry, except the cars are owned by individuals. The drivers apply to be a part of this driving service; and when they are approved, they get a sticker on their car and work whenever they are available. My sister and I had no idea how to get places while we were staying in Los Angeles, so it was nice to put our confidence in drivers who knew the city. I used the app to call for a ride, and the app would tell me who my driver was, what kind of car to expect and how much the ride would cost. The app also provided a map of the journey from our previous destination to the next.

Although I enjoyed this car service and I put my confidence in the driver, I'm also constantly aware that some people like to take advantage of others. This is a sad truth. There will always be those people who manipulate the system for their personal gain. I try not to let one person taint my opinion of the entire system, though. On one occasion, I knew right away that the driver was taking us off course. Sometimes if the paid trip is short, the driver will take a longer, more out-of-the-way route in order to add a few miles to the journey, which will equal a larger payment at the end. I held up my phone and told him that he was going in the opposite direction. I kindly asked him to stay on the course given on my phone. He mumbled under his breath and turned around. I watched my app map the entire drive, and we arrived at our destination in less than five minutes.

Putting our confidence in people doesn't necessarily mean we can't be careful. I want to have a thorough understanding of what and who I'm dealing with before I give over the reins to someone else. Like it was for my twin sister's plastic surgeon, it wasn't until I met him and heard him talk that I felt confident in his ability to help her. When we allow someone to have authority in our lives, we must ensure that they are trustworthy. This doesn't mean that they will be perfect and will never make a mistake. We all make mistakes, and none of us is perfect. However, we can confirm that they are able to do what they say they can do. And once we give them that authority in our lives, we should always have our eyes on God. The Holy Spirit has the map ready for where we need to go. If someone is taking us off course, we will know instantly if our focus is on God. Then we can gently tell them to make the adjustments necessary to get us back on route. And if they won't listen to us, we can ask them to stop the car, so we can find someone who is better suited to get us to where we need to be.

"Trust in the Lord with all your heart; do not depend on your own understanding. Seek his will in all you do, and he will show you which path to take" (Proverbs 3.5-6 NLT).

Father, I don't want to be distrusting, but I do recognize that only You are completely dependable. I know that You will bring people into my life who will help me get to where I need to go, but I also understand that if I keep my eyes on You, You will send me warning flags along the way. I don't expect people to be perfect. I too make mistakes. But I want to have confidence in the people who You send my way. Help me to stay aware of what is going on around me, and guide me with the Truth of Your Word and Your Spirit. I pray this in Jesus' name, amen.

Questions

1. Has God ever sent you warning signs?
2. Are you able to put your confidence in others?
3. Has God used others to bring You closer to His will?

You can put your trust completely in God!

Day 22: Jewel Tone

Wearing Jewel tone colors is extremely important for reality TV. Not only do jewel tones look great on camera, they are also a must while doing interviews in front of the green screen. The only problem is that Christina and I look great in fall colors, and we don't tend to buy a lot of jewel tone clothing—amethyst, sapphire, ruby, citrine, etc. We do, however, like to wear greens, like emerald, but greens are a big "NO" when it comes to the green screen. No green, no white, no black and no busy patterns. Needless to say, I had to go shopping before we went to Los Angeles to film for the show. Although we don't normally wear bright, bold colors, we did so for the show because that is what they needed from us.

The Bible gives us strict life parameters with the Ten Commandments. Also, the Holy Spirit leads us in tailor-made promptings that are for us specifically according to our experience, design and purpose. We may fall short from God's best plan for us, but the grace of God offers second chances. We have freedom through Christ to live for God and chase after His Heart without being subjugated to man-made restrictions of expectation and formality. We become righteous through Christ alone and not through a checklist of religious dos and don'ts (Romans 3.22). The Apostle Paul wanted to bring as many people into heaven as possible. He didn't let menial things prevent Him from reaching others with the Good News of Jesus Christ. Just like Christina and I didn't let a color scheme prevent us from filming the reality show, we don't have to get caught up in preference or taste to the point of causing division.

Some Christians and churches cling onto religious preferences and tastes like they are God's law. They may not be able to reach certain people because they judge others for how they dress, speak or act. Yes, we need to discern right from wrong and teach and obey God's Commandments; but there are some religious traditions that are dividing people when they really shouldn't. What kind of music we play in church, how we dress in church, how we do communion in church and how we give the tithe at church can all be played out differently according to the design of that church. As long as the church teaches that Jesus is God in the flesh come down to earth from heaven to die for the sins of humankind, and He has resurrected to the right-hand side of God, the church is on the right track. We can teach the commandments and the leading of the Holy Spirit while allowing others to live out their walk of faith in a way that expresses who God created them to be.

"When I was with the Jews, I lived like a Jew to bring the Jews to Christ. When I was with those who follow the Jewish law, I too lived under that law. Even though I am not subject to the law, I did this so I could bring to Christ those who are under the law" (1 Corinthians 9.20 NLT).

Father, I don't want to allow basic things, like color scheme, divide me from others. I realize that Your imagination is infinite, and You created each woman and man to be a unique individual. I may not prefer what others prefer, and they may look, dress, talk and act differently, but I still want to love them enough to reach them with the Good News of Jesus Christ. Help me to be able to discern what is Your will from what is human preference. I pray this in Jesus' name, amen.

Questions

1. When have you given allowances for someone's differing preference?
2. Do you see any unnecessary division in the church today?
3. Have you ever given up a personal taste to keep the peace?

We live under grace, not law!

Day 23: Medicine Counter

After our first meeting at the doctor's office before Christina's surgery, a nurse handed us a huge bag of medicine. There were dozens of pills, powders, tablets, ointments and rinses that Christina needed to take or apply. When I spread them out, they completely covered the counter in the kitchen of our hotel room. Some medicines were needed in preparation for surgery. Some were needed the day of the surgery. And most were needed for recovery after the surgery. I was overwhelmed to say the least, but my sister had enough to worry about with having to go through surgery. So I rolled up my sleeves and researched and organized all her meds.

I didn't realize that a single medicine could come in multiple forms and could have multiple uses, so I needed to learn the names, the purposes and the applications of each medicine. Some meds had to be taken before, during or after a meal. Some meds were taken orally, but that same med would be smashed, put in liquid and applied. Some meds were only necessary if the corresponding symptoms developed. Some medicines were for pain, and those had to be carefully monitored. Finally, after much investigation, I came up with a med-taking schedule for my sister. During our two-week stay in Los Angeles, I'd bring her a handful of pills to chug down with water, or I would bring her medicated liquids for her nose or I would bring her Q-tips dipped in ointment. She would simply take or apply what I gave her, trusting that I knew what I was doing.

My sister taking the medicine that I gave her became a beautiful picture of trust. And it was also an awesome image of someone expanding her capacity to meet a need. Many people won't even try to grow in a certain area because they simply say that it's not their strength. Writing is my strength, but God gave me a mind fully capable of learning something new. I am more than a conqueror in Christ. I love my sister, so I became a pharmacist of sorts for a short period of time to help her. Sometimes it is not that we lack skill, resources or aptitude; rather, we could quite simply lack the drive. God will send us people to help and we can rise to the occasion. If He says that we can do it, then we can't let doubt deter us from our destiny. The more we adapt, grow and learn, the greater influence we can have on those around us. The wider we stretch our capacity, the more lives we can touch for Christ.

"No, in all these things we are more than conquerors through him who loved us" (Romans 8.37 NIV).

Father, I don't want to claim defeat in an area that You are calling me to grow. I know it is easier to simply say I can't do it than to try, but I need to make the effort. Give me the motivation I need to rise to the occasion. I believe that I have the Mind of Christ, so I can grow into every area that You are calling me (1 Corinthians 2.16). I want the blessing of filling a need, so I accept the burden of it, knowing that You promise the burden will be light and easy to carry (Matthew 11.30). I pray this in Jesus' name, amen.

Questions

1. Have you ever risen to the occasion?
2. What is something you accomplished that you never dreamed possible?
3. Is there a time you missed a blessing because you claimed defeat?

Rise to the occasion!

Day 24: Favorite Restaurant

Within walking distance of our hotel was a local restaurant. The restaurant's menu was pages thick, so there was a variety of foods to choose from. My sister and I went to the restaurant many times during our two weeks in Los Angeles. We got to know the wait staff. We sat at our regular table. We looked forward to certain foods. It became a safe-haven for us as we were so far from home and displaced from our normal lives. Every time we went, we would end our meal by splitting a dessert and sipping chamomile tea with honey. We took lots of selfies and food pics from that restaurant. We even got postcards from there and sent them to our kids. Today, many of my sweetest memories from my time in Los Angeles with my sister are of us chatting at the restaurant.

The Bible says that God will give us rest. This doesn't mean that we will never find ourselves smack dab in the middle of a trial or hardship. Having surgery was extremely hard for my sister, and being so far from home for two weeks made both our hearts' ache. However, within that storm God did provide us with many moments of rest, including our special times at the restaurant. Many people miss out on their God-ordained rest for different reasons. Maybe they allow their worry to prevent them from resting. Maybe they feel guilty for taking time to rest. Maybe they are focused on things outside of God that they miss His promptings to rest. Whatever the reason is, people can sink during the hard times if they haven't found these platforms of rest.

Especially when we are in a great season of struggle, we need to be seeking times of respite with God. He promises that He will provide rest when we are "weary" and "heavy burdened," but we need to "come to Jesus." My sister and I could have stayed in our hotel room and filled our minds with worry and fear of her surgery, skipping our pre-ordained moments of rest. But we didn't. We knew that we needed something to look forward to. We knew that the days after her surgery we wouldn't be able to leave the hotel room. So we took advantage of the time God was giving us to rest and enjoy each other's company, filling our hearts with memories that would stay with us forever. God is good. He knows that in this life we will experience hard times, which is why He has installed safe havens for our rest and refreshment along the way. We just need to come to Him.

"Then Jesus said, 'Come to me, all of you who are weary and carry heavy burdens, and I will give you rest'" (Matthew 11.28 NLT).

Father, I don't want to miss the moments of rest that You have prepared for me. I trust that You are sending people, places and resources my way that will help me refresh myself before heading back into the storms of life. I want to savor the sweet memories of how You are taking care of me. Don't let worry or distraction cause me to miss out on all the beautiful reprieves You have for me. I pray this in Jesus' name, amen.

Questions

1. When has God ordained a time of rest for you?
2. Have you experienced a time when you were overwhelmed?
3. Did you miss a time of rest because of worry or distraction?

Find your rest!

Day 25: Fixing the Bell Clapper

After my sister's surgery and a few days post-op recovery, a producer planned to visit us at our hotel room and film some "home videos." Christina and I were excited. We were stuck in the hotel for several days while she healed, so it was fun to have something to look forward to. Plus, all the producers were sweet and laidback, so we looked forward to a relaxing chat. The one specification of the producer was to have the bell that I had bought off Rodeo Drive ready to be filmed. They wanted to get a shot of Christina ringing the bell and me coming to her aid. The only problem was that the clapper of the bell came off, and the producer was going to be at our hotel in an hour. I had a choice. I could simply say that the bell broke and we couldn't film it or I could trust that God would get the clapper fixed in an hour. I decided to trust that God would get it fixed.

I knew the surrounding area of our hotel only by a few blocks. I had walked up and down the streets to different location in the near vicinity. I remembered noting a jewelry store on one of my walks because it's door and windows were barred. I had less than an hour to get the bell fixed, grab coffee from the local café and run back to the hotel to take a shower. I didn't know if it was possible, but I was willing to try. I called the jeweler and explained the situation. The woman who answered couldn't quite understand what I meant by a bell, so she asked me to bring it in. I felt kind of silly holding a crystal dinner bell as I entered a jewelry store, but the man wearing the optical visor instantly grabbed my bell and disappeared in the back room. I waited and had no idea if he could fix it or not. About five minutes later, I heard a light jingling sound. The man with the optical visor was ringing the bell and smiling. I couldn't believe it. I thanked him profusely, and when I asked how much I owed him, he shook his head and wouldn't take any money.

I ran with my bell to the café, grabbed our cappuccinos and ran back to the hotel. Did I mention it was raining the entire time? Luckily, the producer had gone to the wrong hotel, so I had an extra fifteen minutes to shower and get ready to be filmed on camera. By the time the producer knocked on our door, I was dressed and ready and had a working bell. I simply had to trust that God would work everything out. God had provided the bell in the first place, and He was going to take care of it. I just needed to have faith and be willing to try. As we take steps of faith, we won't know the outcome. That is why they are called steps of faith. But we can trust that if we do our part of believing and working in that belief that God will do His part of providing for us. Nothing is too hard for God; we simply need to believe and obey.

"And we know that in all things God works for the good of those who love him, who have been called according to his purpose" (Romans 8.28 NIV).

Father, I know that You are watching out for me. You won't abandon me as I take leaps of faith. I know that when I trust you and take a step of obedience, You will establish Your greatest blessings and miracles in my life. Show me how I can move in faith. I want my life to be scattered with stories of Your provision against all odds. Help me to take that step of faith, trusting that You work all things for Your good. I pray this in Jesus' name, amen.

Questions

1. How has God supernaturally provided for you?
2. When have you walked into a dead-end only to see God show up?
3. Do you trust that God can work out all things for your good?

Take a step of faith and watch God provide!

Day 26: Introduction

When filming for a reality show, the production team usually asks that nothing be mentioned on social media before the premier date of the episode. They want to keep everything hush hush in order to save all the excitement for the show. However, people in your life realize that something is going on, especially when you leave for two weeks. So I enjoyed telling those closest to us about God getting Christina on Botched, so she could get her nose deformity fixed. God was about to fulfill the promises that He made to her many years ago. There were always two different reactions from people. Half the people watched the show and became super excited about Christina being one of the patients. The other half, however, did not know the show and seemed confused at first. With the first half, I could discuss the doctors, the patients, going to California and the other details of the show. With the second half, I had to give more of an introduction of the show—the show's premise, how the show helps people, who the doctors were, etc.

I responded differently to the audience with whom I was speaking. Whenever I explained that my sister and I were filming for Botched, I first waited to see the reaction I got. Once I got the reaction, I knew I could either go into the specifics of the show or into the introduction of the show. The introduction took more effort. I had to start from the basics of explaining the reality show first. Moreover, if they weren't aware of my sister's car accident years ago, I had to start from the basics of what happened to her nose. By the time I finally explained the show and my sister's nose deformity, I usually ran out of time to go into further details. As Christians, we should be aware of our audience. We can't simply jump into the specifics of our faith, expecting others to understand us. The Bible says to be ready at all times to give a reason for our hope in Jesus Christ, but we need to identify to whom we are speaking: people who know Christ or People who don't know Christ.

When we are speaking to people who do not know Christ as their Lord and Savior, we will want to launch into an introduction. We will explain how God relates to us through three different Persons--God the Creator (Father), God the Savior (Son, Jesus) and God the Counselor (Holy Spirit, God's Spirit). God made a perfect world for us, but He allowed us to have free will. Free will gives us the choice to love God and create beauty for Him, but with that choice comes the ability to dismiss God and create outside of His will. God knew we would fall short of His glory, so He came into our world in the flesh to redeem our shortcomings. Once we receive Jesus' righteousness, we can now have a relationship with a holy God even in our imperfect state. Proof of this relationship is that we have God's Spirit (the Holy Spirit) living inside of us, guiding us through this life. Once we die, our relationship with God will continue, and we will be with Him forever in eternity (Heaven). But if our audience knows Christ, then we can discuss all the details of faith that encourage us, so they too may be encouraged.

"But in your hearts revere Christ as Lord. Always be prepared to give an answer to everyone who asks you to give the reason for the hope that you have. But do this with gentleness and respect" (1 Peter 3.15 NIV).

Father, I want to be ready at all times to share the hope I have through Jesus Christ. I understand that half my audience may know Jesus, but the other half may not. Let me be ready with my response depending on the reaction of whom I am speaking to. I don't want to dive into details of faith if the person listening doesn't understand what I am talking about. Guide me in truth and let me introduce the name of Jesus Christ with "gentleness and respect," so that people will be open to receive Him as their Lord and Savior. And if the person is already a Christian, let me encourage their faith with all the truths that the Holy Spirit is showing me. I pray this in Jesus' name, amen.

Questions

1. When was the last time you shared your faith?
2. Have you ever introduced Jesus to anyone?
3. What is God teaching you that you can share with others?

Always be prepared!

Day 27: Matching Outfits

I bought my sister and I matching outfits for her surgery. I wanted to show her that I was supporting her even though I couldn't be with her during the eight hours she was under anesthesia. We went to the mall in Los Angeles a few days before her surgery and browsed through the different stores. We finally found comfortable, matching outfits that we could agree on. When we went back to the hotel, I washed all our new clothes. I wanted to make sure the new clothes were extra clean, so Christina wouldn't get an infection on the incisions located on her chest (from the rib removal) and face (from the reconstructive surgery). The next afternoon while my sister was filming her green screen interview, I noticed that I bought myself the wrong size shorts. Since I already washed them, I couldn't return them. I decided to find the store in another location that I could walk to and just buy the same shorts but my size.

The store was a little over two miles from my hotel in the opposite direction of the mall we went to the previous day. I put on my walking shoes, grabbed my headphones and began my walk through Beverly Hills to the store. The day was beautiful and I had so much energy at first. However, half way through, I thought that it would have been a good idea to actually call the store and see if they had the shorts that I needed. I had a sneaking suspicion that my quest for the shorts would be fruitless, but I didn't want to bother with calling. Once I finally got to the store, I could instantly tell that they carried a different variety than the store at the mall. I searched and searched, but my shorts were not there. I couldn't believe it. I had to walk all the way back to the hotel empty handed. I had committed to a Fool's Errand. On the way back, I realized if that I would have called, I could have saved myself the wasted time. My only consolation was that I got a really great workout.

Many times, we set out on a path and don't bother to ask God if our steps will be fruitful. We have a vision of what we want to accomplish in our minds, but we truly can't see beyond the next step in front of us. But there is a God Who sees everything, and He knows if our journey will be profitable or leave us empty handed. Before we forge ahead with our plan, we may want to make sure if the plan is part of God's will. Otherwise, we will get all the way to the end and realize we will have to backtrack our steps. Our views are very limited, and God's ways are higher than our ways. We want to ensure that our path is connected to God's will, so the steps we take can be blessable and bear fruit. If we don't check with God first and get His go-ahead, we may wind up wasting a lot of time. But God is faithful, and He knows that even if we do take the wrong path for a moment, at least we will learn from our mistakes and never make them again.

"For my thoughts are not your thoughts, neither are your ways my ways," declares the LORD. "As the heavens are higher than the earth, so are my ways higher than your ways and my thoughts than your thoughts" (Isaiah 55.8-9 NIV).

Father, I don't want to run ahead of Your will and Your timing. Please remind me to come to You whenever I have a plan. Time is precious, and I don't want to waste a single moment on fruitless journeys. I know that I've made mistakes in the past, and I want to learn from them, so I don't make them again. God, please make sure that all my steps are rooted in You. I know that only acts committed to achieving Your purposes will be divinely blessable and hold eternal value. I pray this in Jesus' name, amen.

Questions

1. Have you ever gone on a "Fool's Errand?"
2. Has God ever told you "no" to a plan of yours?
3. How can you see God's "no" as protection?

Check with God First!

Day 28: Spiritual Attack

When God is in the process of fulfilling His promises, spiritual attacks should be expected. We have an enemy that hates us with a supernatural hatred. We have been made in the image of God, and Satan wants to thwart that image as much as possible (Genesis 1.27). The first thing Satan did after God created Adam and Eve was to sabotage this image by opening their eyes to sin and shame (Genesis 3.7). Satan comes to "steal, kill and destroy," but Jesus came to give us an abundant life (John 10.10). So when Satan sees us walking into God's promises, he pulls out all the stops. Christina and I were far from home, away from family and friends, filming a reality show and receiving God's promises. Of course, the enemy was not happy, so he went into overdrive. Almost every night, we both felt spiritually attacked. We questioned what we said during filming, we longed to be home with our families, we contemplated the ramifications of surgery, etc. We were tempted to be shrouded with doubt, anxiety and fear, and the nights were the hardest because we were tired, weak and alone.

It was during this time that we really leaned into God's Word. We listened to podcasts of several different preachers. We read the Bible together and talked about what we learned. We played Christian music while we slept. We discussed our faith, our promises and what God was doing. We even found an amazing church to attend in Los Angeles. We put forth effort to surround ourselves with God's Word and His Spirit because we were under attack. What Satan meant for evil actually became our good (Genesis 15.20). Instead of falling victim to the enemy's schemes, we actually grew in the Lord and in our faith. We wielded the Sword of Truth and cut off all the lies, deceptions and thieveries that the enemy sent our way. Satan wanted to steal our joy, kill our promises and destroy God's will in our lives. But the Bible says that greater is He that is in us than he that is in the world (1 John 4.4).

When we are walking in God's promises and staying faithful to His will, we must realize that the enemy will attack us. He will attack our minds, hearts and lives. He will do anything and everything to cause mistrust, division, chaos, fear, anxiety, doubt and destruction. But we don't to have to worry about falling prey to his conspiracies. God is on our side, and we have His Truth (the Bible) at our fingertips. During a spiritual attack, we should dig in our heels and lean into God's Word. We live in a time when we have so many resources at our disposal. There is no excuse not to be prepared. We can watch sermons, read Christian books, listen to songs, hear testimonies, attend church, consume God's Word, etc., and receive God's goodness, grace and favor. Plus, we have the Holy Spirit in us Who can manifest God's peace, love, joy and security at any time. Even if there is a spiritual storm raging around us, we can have peace in the eye of the storm because God is protecting us and providing for us.

"But you belong to God, my dear children. You have already won a victory over those people, because the Spirit who lives in you is greater than the spirit who lives in the world" (1 John 4.4 NLT).

Father, I know that You are more powerful than my enemy, and you will give me everything I need to be victorious. I won't be surprised when I come under spiritual attack, especially when I am in the middle of God fulfilling His great promises for my life. When I feel lost and alone, I will lean into Your Word and goodness. I will not let doubt, fear, worry and anxiety consume me, and I will protect my faith in Your promises. I believe that You created me in Your image, and I won't let the enemy fill me with shame. I pray this in Jesus' name, amen.

Questions

1. When have you been under spiritual attack?
2. What helped you through this difficult time?
3. How can you use the resources around you to keep your faith?

God will help you overcome!

Day 29: Staying Behind

My husband felt God prompting him five years ago to open his own business. Anyone who has ever delved into entrepreneurial territory knows just how difficult this venture truly is. Just when he decided to take the leap of faith, he was offered a promotion at work. It seems to always happen like that: when we step out onto God's promises, we always get tempted to compromise our faith. My husband resisted the temptation to forfeit what God was stirring in his heart. For about two years, he had to work two jobs. He worked full time at his current job and full time at his fledgling business. During this time, I pulled my two older kids out of school and kept all three of them at home. I decided to continue homeschooling during this busy season. Otherwise, our kids would rarely see their father. He worked every day of the week except for the one day he switched from night to day shift. Since I decided to homeschool, we would all drive to see him for lunch almost every day.

I trusted what God was doing in my husband's life, so I took up the slack at home. I became, in essence, a single mom for two years. I knew this time wouldn't last long, and I was willing to do what was necessary for his business and our family to thrive. Five years later, my husband and I own several businesses, which are all doing well. Now he can be home much more often. The sacrifice was worth it in the end. Just recently, I needed to help my sister. Leaving for two weeks was difficult, but my husband knew that God was leading me on a journey towards His promises. So my husband willingly became a single dad for two weeks while I was gone. He did what was necessary for me to help my sister recover from surgery. My husband and I both sacrifice to ensure that our family is protected and nurtured, and we both receive the blessings that are included in each other's steps of faith. This reminds me of an incident with King David from the Old Testament.

The Amalekites had kidnaped the wives and children of David and his men. They instantly set out to rescue their families. About midway in their journey, some of the men were to the point of exhaustion. David and his men decided to leave their supplies, and the men left behind watched over everything. After the wives and children were rescued and much plunder was taken, some of the "wicked" men didn't want to share what God had given them. But David set a precedent. He determined that whoever stayed behind to guard the stuff while the others fought the battle would get equal share of the plunder. That's how I feel about when I stayed home when my husband started the business, and when he stayed home so I could help my sister. Whether we stayed home to protect our family or went off to fight the battle, we each receive equal parts of the blessings. His victories are my victories and my victories are his.

"Who will listen to what you say? The share of the man who stayed with the supplies is to be the same as that of him who went down to the battle. All will share alike" (1 Samuel 30.24 NIV).

Father, I know that I won't always be the one who gets to leave home and fight the battles of faith. But staying behind and protecting the home front is just as important as fighting. Both fighting and protecting take faith, strength and commitment. I can share in the battles of my spouse, knowing that we each took different but important roles. Lord, help my spouse and I to fully enjoy the blessings that we each receive. I pray this in Jesus' name, amen.

Questions

1. When have you stayed behind?
2. Do you enjoy the rewards of your spouse's victory?
3. Has someone stayed behind, so you could walk in faith?

We all share alike!

Day 30: Oasis Church

My sister and I didn't know much about Los Angeles. Every store, restaurant and destination was new to us. We weren't familiar with any local churches either. Thankfully, our home church had a women's conference several years back, and a pastor's wife from Los Angeles was one of the speakers. I remembered the speaker's name and looked up the church. It was less than ten miles away from our hotel, so we requested a ride to attend church. It was the day before my twin sister's surgery, and I knew we needed to find encouragement and hope from the Body of Christ.

We got to church early, so we could see the staff and volunteers get ready. I was surprised by how young and hip the church members were. They each layered stylish pieces of trendy ensemble – scarves, hats, vests, jewelry. My sister and I wore simple outfits, and we actually felt old fashioned in our jeans and long sleeve t-shirts. The youthful church family seemed a contradiction to the old cathedral where they held church, but the energy brought the antique building to life. And I realized that God loves to breathe life into old, out-of-date things. He can show off His glory and transform dry desert land into a prosperous Oasis. I looked around me that day and experienced energy and vitality within a building that would have been dead and barren.

I wonder how many times we miss out on God's blessings because we automatically mark something in our lives as dead and barren. We have no faith in the renewal of the emptiness within and around us, so we don't give God the opportunity to produce new life in wilderness. We limit God because we have forgotten that He specialized in bringing the dead back to life and producing abundance from within the void. We have to look around and ask ourselves if there is a dream, desire or promise that has remained dormant and been forgotten. God-given dreams do not die. Though they may look dead in the natural, Jesus is whispering, "No, it's just asleep, but I am ready to wake it up" (John 11.11). We have to believe in the Resurrection Power of Jesus Christ and trust that God loves bringing His energy and vitality into our barrenness.

"Then he said to me, "Speak a prophetic message to these bones and say, 'Dry bones, listen to the word of the LORD! This is what the Sovereign LORD says: Look! I am going to put breath into you and make you live again!" (Ezekiel 37.4-5 NLT).

Father, I don't want to let the desires of my heart to lay dormant forever because I haven't put faith in Your ability to bring them back to life. I know that nothing is impossible for You. You give life to dry bones, You form rivers in the desert and You can resurrect the dead. I put my faith in Your Word and not my circumstances. Bring to my mind any areas of my life that I have allowed to stay desolate. I believe that You can bring joy into my pain, energy into the emptiness and life into the deadness of my dreams. I pray this in Jesus' name, amen.

Questions

1. Are there any dormant dreams in your life?
2. Have you overlooked areas that God wants to use?
3. Do you believe in the Resurrection Power of Jesus Christ?

Let Jesus wake up your promises!

Day 31: Communion

After my sister's surgery, we did not leave the hotel much. For the first three days, I stayed with her the entire time only leaving to buy us coffee from the café just down the street. Around the fourth day, we could walk to our favorite restaurant only a few blocks away. But getting into a car and going sightseeing was definitely not an option. I had hoped that we could go to church the second week we were there, but it just wasn't possible. Christina had a large bandage on her nose and traveling fatigued her. So we decided we would listen to a sermon via Podcast and do communion together. I kept some bread from one of our meals and grabbed a grape-blend juice box from the café. We listened to a two-part sermon about communion and ate the bread and drank the juice together.

Communion is a symbolic reminder of what Jesus came to earth to achieve. His body was like the bread, broken to pour out God's love, grace and Spirit into the natural world from heaven. His blood was like wine, the Living Water of God mixed with flesh of the earth to redeem the world and reconcile all of us back to God. In communion, we are given the mysterious image of John 3.16: "For God so loved the world that he gave his one and only Son, that whoever believes in him shall not perish but have eternal life" (NIV). Jesus is God in the flesh and Lord over the Sabbath. God created all the earth and humanity in six days, and He gave us free will to create for His glory. He knew that we could create evil, but He had already installed a redemption plan. He prepared the Seventh Day of Creation, knowing that the final day would redeem the entire week back to Him. It would be the seventh day that Jesus would die and rise again, executing a shockwave of healing, redemption and reconciliation across space and time.

We take communion in remembrance of what Jesus has done for us. We can rest from our striving to be perfect, knowing that Jesus has given us His perfection. He took our sins to the grave and left them there before rising back to life. The Bible says that He freely gave His life, but He had the authority to take back His life. Paul affirms in Hebrews that we should strive to enter into the rest that is rightfully ours through Jesus Christ (Hebrews 4.11). Our rest is the redemption and reconciliation of the Finished Work of Jesus on the Cross. He worked on Sabbath, so we could rest in the cross. We take communion to remember that we have rest. We have been forgiven. Our efforts have been redeemed. We can create for God's glory on earth, knowing that the Blood of Jesus Christ makes it all pleasing to God.

"No one takes it from me, but I lay it down of my own accord. I have authority to lay it down and authority to take it up again. This command I received from my Father" (John 10.18 NIV).

Father, I realize that because I have asked Jesus Christ to be my Lord and Savior that my life has been redeemed and I am reconciled back to God. God gave me free will, knowing that I would fall short of His glory, but He already had a redemption plan prepared. I can rest from always trying to earn my way into heaven and into God's presence. I have the Holy Spirit inside of me even in my imperfect state because of the Finished Work of Jesus Christ on the Cross. I can have Sabbath every day, truly finding rest in the Seventh Day of Creation Week. Thank You, Lord, for loving me so much that You would die for me. I take communion to remember that Your body was broken and Your blood spilled to bring me back into fellowship with God. I pray this in Jesus' name, amen.

Questions

1. What does the Blood and Bread mean to you?
2. How can you add communion into your life?
3. Do you strive to enter into the rest of Sabbath?

Incorporate communion into your life!

Day 32: Laughing Pains

My sister had a portion of her rib taken out for her nose surgery. The doctors needed the rib, so they could harvest the cartilage to reconstruct her nose. The interesting reality about her nose surgery was that the rib extraction hurt the most. For the first several days, she couldn't sit up in bed without me helping her. Not only did inside her chest cavity ache where the rib was taken, but the incision on the skin above her ribs hurt, as well. The pain of her nose lessened each day, but weeks later her chest still hurts. What was worse is that during the first week of recovery, everything seemed comical to my sister. This caused me to say and do things that made her laugh. I really didn't mean to be funny, but as she tried and tried not to laugh, the situation became more and more hilarious to where I was buckled over in laughter.

The irony of mixing laughter with pain can be good medicine. Although it hurt for my sister to laugh, the effects of laughter actually help her feel better. Laughter decreases hormones that cause stress, and they increase antibodies that fight infection. Laughter also activates endorphins, the body's natural feel good chemicals. These chemicals offer the body pain relief and a sense of happiness. Though my sister complained while she was laughing, the effects of her laughter really helped the process of recovery. I don't doubt that it was her feeling of well-being and security that encouraged her body to heal as quickly as it did. In fact, the doctor was so impressed on how well Christina's body was recovering that we got to go home early. The laughter she suffered through ignited the chemicals and antibodies that her body needed to heal.

The Bible literally says that a "cheerful heart is good medicine." It is no surprise to me that the Bible knew something thousands of years ago that science is just now discovering today. When we are physically or emotionally hurt, the best way to help the healing process along is to laugh. It may seem ironic, and it may seem wrong to seek out laughter when the heart hurts and the body is broken, but that is exactly what is needed. My sister's pain was real, and there were times she cried because of it; but when God opens the doors for her to laugh, she was able to produce chemicals in her body that brought her greater healing. This is a reminder to us. When we feel hurt, heavy with burdens or physically wounded, we must surround ourselves by people and situations that will encourage the healing of laughter. We cannot allow a broken spirit to steal our strength and restrict our recovery. God will send laughter our way, but we must be willing to cheer up.

"A cheerful heart is good medicine, but a broken spirit saps a person's strength" (Proverbs 17.22 NLT).

Father, I don't want to hold onto my pain and bitterness any longer. I want to heal both physically and emotionally, so I will make myself available to laugh. It does feel awkward trying to be cheerful when I hurt so much, but I know that my body will release chemicals that will help my heart, mind and body recover faster. Please send people my way who can cheer me up and surround me in situations that will induce laughter. I want to feel better again. I pray this in Jesus' name, amen.

Questions

1. Have you ever laughed during a difficult time?
2. Do you feel okay with finding joy in your pain?
3. Who in your life is able to make you laugh?

A cheerful heart can heal!

Day 33: Fig Tree

The night after my sister's reconstructive nose surgery, I stayed in a room next to hers at the recovery hospital. Before I went to bed, I opened the Bible and started reading from the Book of Mark. I read how Jesus was hungry, so He went to the fig tree, anticipating a few figs to eat. Although the fig tree had many green leaves, it was not the season for fruit. Jesus then cursed the fig tree to never grow fruit again, and a day later the disciples noticed that the fig tree had withered and died from the roots up. I remembered reading these verses over and over again. I thought it was unfair that Jesus wanted fruit from a tree when figs were not in season. I imagined Jesus and the fig tree facing each other, and I heard God ask me one simple question: "Which one is more powerful? The Word of Jesus or the season of the fig tree?" I knew exactly what God was teaching me. The will of Jesus usurps our natural circumstances. If Jesus wants fruit in an area of our lives that goes against the order of things, the Word of Jesus will always win.

In the Bible, there are many stories of God moving outside the natural systems that He created on this earth. Sarah gave birth in her old age (Genesis 21). Moses split the Red Sea (Exodus 14). Joshua asked the sun to stand still (Joshua 10). Isaiah turned back time (Isaiah 38). And Peter healed Tabitha (Acts 9). God performed supernatural miracles through normal, everyday people. God is not restricted by situations, circumstances or seasons. If God's Word and a natural circumstance face off, God will win every time. However, when God wants to perform these miracles through us, we must have the receiver for His power: FAITH. We must have faith that God is stronger than our circumstances. When we have faith in God's promises even when they are out of season, God will produce the fruit of His Word in our lives.

After Jesus cursed the fig tree, Peter noticed that it had died. When he asked Jesus about the tree, Jesus responded with an illustration of faith. He explained that if we have faith to tell a mountain to be thrown into the sea, it would be done. All we have to do is believe (Mark 11.23). A mountain going into the sea is an excellent example of God moving outside of the natural circumstances that He created. We might be facing many natural circumstances that tell us that God's promises can never happen. But it doesn't matter how impossible the situation seems, God can do the impossible if we have faith that His Word is stronger than the season we find ourselves in. When we are confronted with putting our trust in Jesus' Word versus putting our trust in the emptiness of our situation, we should always bank all our faith on the impossible!

"I tell you, you can pray for anything, and if you believe that you've received it, it will be yours" (Mark 11.24 NLT).

Father, I have more faith in Your promises for my life than the impossible circumstances that I find myself in. You move outside of the systems that You have created in order to produce miracles that shine Your glory. Let me be an example like so many people in the Bible of how You move in miracles. I want people to look at my life and see You producing impossible fruit out of season. I have faith in Your Word to fulfill every promise for my life You have given me despite the natural circumstances that try to stifle my dreams. Help me to put more faith in You than in my situation on earth. I pray this in Jesus' name, amen.

Questions

1. Do you have impossible promises today?
2. Is God stronger than your circumstances?
3. How can you bank your faith on God's Word?

God can move mountains in your life!

Day 34: Overweight Bags

The day before my sister and I flew back home from Los Angeles, we went through the process of packing. We bought a few matching outfits and several gifts for family and friends during the two weeks we were gone, so we wanted to make sure that our bags weren't overweight. If they were even a pound too heavy, we would be charged an extra hundred dollars each by the airline. Since we were in Los Angeles for so long, we had one large suitcase that we would check in and one smaller suitcase that we would stow in the overhead compartments on the plane. The hotel had a suitcase scale in the lobby, so we each brought our large bags downstairs to weigh. On our first trip to the scale, Christina's bag was just a few pounds underweight and mine was about five pounds over. We went back upstairs to reorganize our bags.

I pulled stuff out of my bag, and she put some into hers. Then I tried to shove some items into my smaller bag, but it was already stuffed to the max. After we shuffled things around, we brought the bags downstairs to the scale. Now my suitcase was right at the limit and Christina's was overweight. We brought the suitcases upstairs again, and this time we had to figure something else out. I remembered that I had brought two small backpacks on the trip just in case we needed them, so we decided to use them as carry-ons. We moved around items in our bags one more time, and placed smaller items into our backpacks. Finally, we went downstairs a third time. This time both our bags were a few pounds underweight. We had made it just under capacity. We each had one large suitcase, one small suitcase, one carryon and one purse. I didn't think it was possible, but somehow we were able to pack everything within regulation restrictions.

Many times, God wants us to reach our full capacity before He moves us to the next level. We are unable to move forward in our current situation, but instead of just supernaturally providing a breakthrough, He expects us to stretch our capacity first. God won't provide a miracle if we still have room to grow. While we are waiting for God to give us a bigger suitcase, He's waiting for us to pull out the small backpack that we have forgotten about. He knows that when we move to the next level, we can use the backpack to accomplish a bigger version of His Kingdom Plan for our lives. Instead of waiting on God to provide, we should look around us for any resources that we already have in our possession. It is not until we stretch and grow to capacity that God will finally provide for us. We must do everything we can do in the natural, so God can do His supernatural.

"Enlarge the place of your tent, stretch your tent curtains wide, do not hold back; lengthen your cords, strengthen your stakes" (Isaiah 54.2 NIV).

Father, I know that there is more room for me to learn and grow. I don't want You to move on my behalf until I've exhausted every effort in stretching my capacity. Show me the resources around me that I can use to "lengthen my cords." Guide me into areas that I can expand to be used for Your glory. I do want a miracle in my life, and I do want You to provide the supernatural. But I also want to do as much as I can do in the natural before You move me into the next level of my walk of faith. I pray this in Jesus' name, amen.

Questions

1. Are there areas that you can grow?
2. Do you have resources that you may be neglecting?
3. How can you stretch the cords of your capacity today?

Do the natural, so God can do the supernatural!

Day 35: Broken, Bound & Healed

Christina's nose went through a lot of transformations over many years after her car accident. At first the damage done to her nose was not noticeable, but over several years the twisting inside and outside of her nose began to show. She had her first nose surgery about six years after her car accident. Then her nose looked okay for a short while, but several months later, her nose began to twist even more than before. By the time I sent her application in to Botched, it had been about five years since her first nose surgery, and eleven years since her car accident. That's a long time to deal with a problem. Her nose needed surgery one more time. Not just a simple surgery. She needed an eight-hour surgery with several doctors and nurses. She needed to give up a portion of her rib and deal with a grueling recovery. Her nose had been deformed for so long that the doctors needed to undo the damage and correct the problem.

Her nose had to endure the final process of being broken, bound and healed. Although they didn't literally break her nose, they still had to crack a rib in half, cut open her nose, shave down some bone and reconstruct the cartilage. Luckily, she slept during this process or she would have been in extreme pain. Once they were done with surgery, they bound her nose, so it could heal. Finally, after so many years of dealing with her twisting nose, she could recover in confidence that her nose would be whole once more. This process not only applies to us physically, but spiritually. God sometimes has to break us down in order to build us back up again in His best design for us.

The word, broken, is used a lot in the Bible. It is actually a very beautiful and powerful word that brings forth healing, strength and wholeness. God is shaping us into the image of Jesus, and often we have deep rooted problems that are "twisting" us from the best design God has for us. Because God loves us, He will break us and bind us, so we can heal in God's strength and overcome any spiritual deformity that life has caused in us. All of us have been injured by people and circumstances, and if we don't know to seek help right away, the injury can worsen and affect every aspect of our lives. God will allow us to be broken under His careful hand, so He can make us right again. We must not be afraid of being broken. The process is painful, but we can trust that God will bind us up right away, so we can heal. And once the bandages come off, we will walk in a higher victory with the Lord.

"Come, let us return to the LORD. He has torn us to pieces but he will heal us; he has injured us but he will bind up our wounds" (Hosea 6.1 NIV).

Father, I don't want to run away from the brokenness that You have placed before me. I know walking into hardships and trials will be painful, but I trust that You are walking alongside of me. I must be broken, so You can correct injuries in my life that are trying to twist my purpose and design. I know that You will bandage my hurt, and after a time of rest, I will heal into a greater authority and victory with You. I know You care about me, and You want to form me into the best design that You have created. I pray this in Jesus' name, amen.

Questions

1. Has God walked you through a time of brokenness?
2. Once you healed, did you claim a bigger victory?
3. Can you see God using hardships to shape you?

God breaks, but He also heals!

Day 36: Writing Devotionals

Although I wrote a lot in college and as an English teacher, I didn't start writing about faith until I was in my late twenties. When I started writing about God, I felt unworthy. I asked God by what authority did I have to write about spiritual matters, and He answered back that He gave me the authority. I don't have a theology degree, but the Holy Spirit has been homeschooling me in His Truth for many years now. Nothing is better than having the Holy Spirit as your personal Teacher, Mentor and Guide. I wrote my Christian Fiction book first between the ages of twenty-eight and twenty-nine, and God allowed it to sit on the backburner for many years. During my early thirties, I began writing devotionals. So far I've written hundreds of devotionals, along with my other fiction and nonfiction books. I once thought that my devotional writing was not as important as my other fiction and nonfiction writing, but I have since realized that there is great value in devotionals.

Devotionals are usually short and easy to read. I like to compare them to the granola bar of spiritual writing. You can grab a quick devotional and find enough sustenance to give you a spiritual boost during your day. They connect a reality with a spiritual truth, which gives readers a deeper revelation that is applicable to their lives. I know that I love reading devotionals because they help me to meditate on God and His Word. I have a stack of devotionals written by both men and women. Some were written hundreds of years ago, and others were written only a few years ago. And it never fails that God is able to use those writers' words to encourage me in my current situation. If I feel even the slightest emotions of worry, doubt or fear; I will open up a devotional and read it.

Although the Bible is the most important Book of all, devotionals are valuable because they demonstrate *devotion* to the Lord and His Word. Every devotional I write, I'm leaning on the Lord to show me what He wants me to say. Sometimes, I have no idea what spiritual truth I will convey, but God never fails to give me a small revelation as I take a step to write by faith. Some people regard devotionals as too simplistic with not enough substance in them. But if you consume a devotional every day, the insights you glean will add up. And after a year of reading devotionals, you will have gained a buffet of appetizing spiritual nuggets. My husband and I read devotionals to our kids every day. I just think of them as spiritual packs of nutrition, preparing them for a victorious day and life. Devotionals are amazing for people just starting their walks of faith and for people who have been walking with the Lord for decades. We don't need theology degrees to read or write them. We simply need a desire to understand and know God and to grow in our relationship with Him.

"But they delight in the law of the LORD, meditating on it day and night. They are like trees planted along the riverbank, bearing fruit each season. Their leaves never wither, and they prosper in all they do" (Psalm 1.2-3 NLT).

Father, I want to meditate on You and Your Word. I know that the Bible is by far the most essential book of all, but I do want to see through the eyes of other Believers and taste the revelations You have shown them. I receive a more dynamic understanding of You when I can gather up various perspectives of people who love You. I ask that You bring to me devotionals that will encourage me in the season of life that I find myself. Show me how to see You in every area of my life. I pray this in Jesus' name, amen.

Questions

1. What are some of your favorite devotional books?
2. How has a devotional helped you?
3. What spiritual truth have you gleaned from a devotional?

Let a devotional snack give you a spiritual boost!

Day 37: Seven Ladies

I organized the attendees for my sister's Los Angeles reveal of her new nose. I wanted the moment to be special. She had been dealing with this issue for so long, and God had shown up so powerfully that I knew I had to make the reveal special. So many family and friends pulled together for Christina and me to go to California to film the episode and for Christina to have surgery, and I wanted to express my gratitude to everyone involved. I wanted all of us to celebrate everything that God had done. I rallied five women to attend my sister's reveal in California along with my twin and me, so we had seven ladies in all. The ladies included both family and friends and several of them lived in different cities and states. I became the liaison between the producers and the reveal ladies. I helped organize plane tickets, hotel plans and wardrobe. I made a mass text to all the ladies, and thus began the fine-tuning of the event.

The airline tickets may have been the hardest to arrange. I wanted to make sure the ladies would be meeting at around the same time at the Los Angeles Airport, but I was flying them in from three different locations. I kind of felt like Scotty from Star Trek beaming three people from three different locations onto the same platform. The process took a few days, several calls and more emails to the ladies and producers, but we finally scheduled the flights. The hotel was another issue. I needed to know the location of the hotel, how many rooms we would need and who would be staying with whom; but after a week, we ultimately got everything arranged. Lastly, and most importantly, I needed to arrange the wardrobe. Since the theme of the reveal was "garden lunch," we decided to go with a spring and floral look. The biggest tragedy to happen at any event would be for two ladies to wear the same dress. Therefore, I had all the ladies send in photos of what they would be wearing. It's interesting to note that the wardrobe mass text would be the longest thread of all. Getting diverse women to come together on wardrobe is a monumental feat, but we did it!

My sister had no idea about all the details that went into planning her reveal. I kept her from the mass texts, emails and phone calls because I wanted to her not to worry about a single thing. It was as if I was throwing a birthday party in honor of her new nose, so she didn't have to deal with all the particulars. As coordinator, it could have been easy to become lost in the details, opinions, delays and snags of planning, but I've learned not to get anxious. I trust that God will pour into my efforts and make sure everything works out in the end. If God has placed us in a leadership position, we must learn not to sweat the small stuff. If we let every snag or delay frustrate us, we will never come into an event with joy and peace. Yes, we know all the details, but we can't let them cause us to worry or fret. There must be a sense that God is the ultimate Leader and nothing passes His eyes unseen. He sees everything, and if He's not anxious, we shouldn't be either. God gives leadership positions to people who He knows will not lose their peace and joy. When the details try to steal your joy, simply do what you can do and let God take care of the rest.

"The LORD is my strength and shield. I trust him with all my heart. He helps me, and my heart is filled with joy. I burst out in songs of thanksgiving" (Psalm 28.7 NLT).

Father, I want You to be able to trust me in a leadership role. I realize now that leadership is actually about serving. I want to serve others with joy and peace, and I will not let the little things that go wrong to trip me up. I will trust that You are the final Authority, and You are working through my obedience to achieve something greater than I can accomplish on my own. Even though I may be aware of all snags and delays, I won't let them cause me to be anxious or frustrated. I pray this in Jesus' name, amen.

Questions

1. What leadership position do you serve in?
2. Do you allow the details to steal your peace?
3. How can you keep your joy by trusting God?

Don't sweat the details!

Day 38: The Necklace

I wanted to find my twin sister a gift for her reveal that embodied her struggle through the years, culminating into a really tough year of divorce and nose deformity. I also wanted that gift to display God's goodness in redeeming her and fulfilling His long-awaited promises for her life. I prayed about it, and went straight to Etsy to find a handmade gift that would stand as a symbolic manifestation of the physical and emotional transformation that my sister has undergone. After a few minutes of searching, I found a necklace with the verse from Psalm 147.3 written on it: *"He heals the brokenhearted and binds up their wounds."* This verse expresses that God heals both our physical and emotional brokenness simultaneously. So many times, physical and emotional pain go hand in hand. The faucets of our being are so closely wired that it is truly difficult to have one and not the other. Emotional pain can manifest physical symptoms, and physical trauma can wreak havoc on our emotional state.

God knows this. He came into this earth as a baby and walked among us. He was called Emmanuel, God with us, and He was God in the flesh, Jesus Christ. His body was broken for us, and His Spirit was in despair because He was separated from the Father. Jesus took our sins, so God had to look away from His One and Only Son for a time. He was forsaken by the Father, so we would never have to be Forsaken. Jesus experienced both physical and emotional pain and death, so He could walk with us during our suffering. Jesus took on the sins of the world, so His joy, peace and wholeness could prevail over humanity. We no longer have to experience the pain of death—eternal separation from God—because Jesus carried our sins into the grave. But He resurrected three days later, leaving our sin behind.

We may have become accustomed to the idea that Jesus came into the earth to die on the cross and reconcile us back to God because of His great love, but this story is the best and truest Love Story of all time. Every love story that people try to create are only whispers and shadows of the Greatest Love Story ever told. We are loved by our Creator. He is perfect, and we are not. But instead of allowing our separation by sin to permeate, He took our sin and gave us His righteousness. The only way God could do that was to leave His Heavenly throne, put on flesh, enter this earth and take our separation. Jesus experienced both physical and emotional pain on our behalf. He loves us, and He walks with us during our times of pain and heartache. We don't have to despair because Jesus has given us His Healing, Grace, Favor, Peace, Joy and Wholeness. All we need to do is reach up to Him and grasps all that is good.

"Surely He took up our pain and bore our suffering, yet we considered Him punished by God, stricken by Him, and afflicted. But He was pierced for our transgressions, He was crushed for our iniquities; the punishment that brought us peace was on Him, and by His wounds we are healed" (Isaiah 53.4-5 NIV).

Father, thank You for sending Your Son, Jesus Christ, into this world to die for our sins. I know that I'm not alone in my affliction and heartache. Jesus died, so that God's Spirit could walk down difficult and painful roads with me. I release my hurts to You, and I know that You are healing me both emotionally and physically. You were wounded, so I could be healed. You were forsaken, so I would never be alone. I can be with God in heaven because You took my sins to the grave and left them there. Thank You for dying on the Cross for me. I don't ever want to take Your death and resurrection for granted. I pray this in Jesus name, amen.

Questions

1. Do you know that your sins have been forgiven?
2. How did Jesus reconcile you back to God?
3. Have you asked Jesus to be your Lord and Savior?

Jesus heals the body and heart!

Day 39: Facetime

A few weeks after we returned home from my sister's nose surgery, I noticed that I missed a Facetime call from her. I dismissed the call, believing that she must have called me by accident because we have never Facetimed each other before. Then a few day later, I received another Facetime call from her. She's a morning person and I am not. She wakes up in a great mood and full of energy, and I wake up having to choke down my melancholy personality. I literally have to tell myself: "This is the day the Lord has made, so I will rejoice and be glad in it (Psalm 118.24). I grabbed my phone wondering if something was wrong since it was so early in the morning. I accepted the call and watched and listened to my sister as she commenced to ramble on with enthusiasm. I don't recall what she was talking about, but it became obvious that it wasn't very important. I remember thinking that she was way too lively for so early in the morning. While she was all smiles, I was still bleary-eyed.

About five minutes later, we got off the phone. I hung up the Facetime and stared at the screen. That's when the thought struck me that we have never Facetimed. I remembered the call I missed from her a few days ago. Maybe it wasn't an accident. Why has my twin all of a sudden taken to Facetime? I'm an introvert, so text usually suits me best. What had changed? That's when I realized that my sister's nose wasn't deformed anymore. Although she probably didn't realize it, her deformity caused her to change what would come naturally to her. She never Facetimed me because she was self-conscious about her nose. The progression was slow, but her everyday choices and actions were drastically altered by her deformity. Now that God had healed her, she was able to be who God designed her to be: an extrovert who likes to Facetime.

God has His best design for each of us. Sometimes this design gets altered by the blows of the world. People and situations hurt us, and we slowly get used to the pain until it becomes normal. We may not think the pain has altered our life, but it truly has. We may be missing the fullness of who God created us to be because we won't let God deal with our wounds. But when we finally seek healing and go through the process of recovery, we will enthusiastically jump into the freedom of who we were created to be. Having God do surgery on our hearts, minds and emotions may seem scary, but the life-changing freedom on the other side is worth the effort, humility and risk. God has His best design and best life waiting for us. We just need to let Him into the scarred and wounded parts of our lives. He knows this world isn't perfect. He knows that we will be hurt and damaged along the way. But He is fully capable and prepared to bring victory into our pain because He knows that we will come out stronger, freer and more grateful for how we have been designed.

"So Christ has truly set us free. Now make sure that you stay free, and don't get tied up again in slavery to the law" (Galatians 5.1 NLT).

Father, I want to walk in the freedom of my best design. I have experienced blows in this life, but I do not want my pain and heartache to alter who You created me to be. In fact, I want my hardships to propel me into my best self. But I know that I need to let You work in my life, exposing my wounds and healing them. I won't be embarrassed. I want to humble myself and ask for Your help because I know on the other side of my recovery will be joy, peace and freedom. I don't want to grow accustomed to living beneath my purpose. Create in me a passion to embrace the fullness of what You have for me. I pray this in Jesus' name, amen.

Questions

1. Is there a wound that is limiting your life?
2. Does God need to do some healing in you?
3. What freedom does God have on the other side of recovery?

Christ has set you free!

Day 40: Pray and Run

My twin sister and I were under great spiritual attack when we were trying to get to her Botched Reveal in Los Angeles. I had already coordinated five other women to be there—our mom, our older sister, my sister-in-law and two friends. They flew into California earlier, and they were anxiously awaiting our arrival. When Christina and I got to the airport for the first leg of our flight, it became obvious that circumstances were rising to stop us from reaching our destination. From a hailstorm in Dallas to misspelled names on our tickets, the process of getting to Los Angeles went from one setback to the next and from one miracle to the next.

Our first flight was delayed to the next morning, so we got three hours of sleep and arrived at the airport at 3.30 in the morning. We had to make each flight on our way to Los Angeles because our family and friends were leaving the following morning. There was no room for delays. As we were flying into Dallas, we realized that our next flight was already boarding. I texted my husband, asking him to please pray. I remember what he wrote back: "I'm praying, but run!" My sister and I grabbed our luggage and ran through the airport to another terminal, catching our flight just before it was taking off. We arrived so late that they were in the process of giving my seat to someone on standby. If we had not run, no prayer could have gotten us on that plane.

Many times we want a miracle from God, but we forget that we must run as well as pray. Praying is monumental. Prayer is our ability to access God's Kingdom Plan and shape the future with our faith. However, prayer is not enough…. we must act by faith on our prayer. God provided my sister and I just enough time to catch our next flight within the parameters of us giving Him our best effort. In this life, we can run for God, knowing that He will erupt a miracle from efforts. We can pray for a miracle while at the same time running by faith towards that miracle.

"Don't be afraid, for I am with you. Don't be discouraged, for I am your God. I will strengthen you and help you. I will hold you up with my victorious right hand" (Isiah 41.10 NLT).

Father, I know that You have given many promises, and I have been praying for them to be established. But I realize now that I also need to run towards them by faith. My belief will get me moving. My disbelief will make me stagnant. I want to chase after my destiny, knowing that You will bless my efforts and provide miracles to every setback along the way. Show me how to rest in You while moving my feet. I want to pray and run after my God-given dreams. I pray this in Jesus' name, amen.

Questions

1. What are a few of God's promises for your life?
2. How can you move by faith towards your destiny?
3. Have you been stagnant in chasing your dreams?

Pray but run!

Thank you for following me on this writing journey. I hope you enjoyed this devotional book. May you be filled with the love of our Creator, the wisdom of our Counselor and the courage of our Savior.

If you would like to read any of my other books, check out my Amazon Page. You can find me at alisahopewagner.com, Facebook, Twitter, YouTube, Instagram and Goodreads. My social media handle is @alisahopewagner.

If you enjoyed this book, I would very much appreciate a review on Amazon. Scroll under the reviews and click "Write a Customer Review." Give your stars and a few words of encouragement!